Also by Jenny La Sala:

Comes A Soldier's Whisper

Vietnam and Beyond, Veteran Reflections

When Daddy Comes Home

Never Forgotten, The Vietnam
Veteran Fifty Years Later

When Mommy Comes Home

A Leap of Faith

The Men and Women Who Served Post 9/11

Jenny La Sala

Order this book online at www.trafford.com
or email orders@trafford.com

Most Trafford titles are also available at major online book retailers.

Print information available on the last page.

ISBN: 978-1-4907-9222-4 (sc)
ISBN: 978-1-4907-9221-7 (hc)
ISBN: 978-1-4907-9223-1 (e)

Library of Congress Control Number: 2018913685

Trafford rev. 12/22/2018

 www.trafford.com

North America & international
toll-free: 1 888 232 4444 (USA & Canada)
fax: 812 355 4082

CONTENTS

FOREWORD

" *A lso I heard the voice of the Lord, saying, Whom shall I send, and who will go for us? Then said I, Here am I; send me.*"
Isaiah 6:8, KJV

What can any of us give to those who have offered themselves as our shield against the greatest dangers we face in the world? What indeed, can any of us do to comfort those whose wounds may or may not be visible, but the pain and unanswered questions they now carry in their soul can be seen etched on their faces and written into their changed demeanor? How can any of us help those who have stood in harm's way on our behalf, while today, many of these Heroes find themselves facing the solitude of silent anguish as their new, constant companion because of memories they can't erase?

Jenny La Sala gives us an answer in her stirring book, "A Leap of Faith." She awakens us to the role each of us has in caring for those who have survived the battlefield. In doing so, she reminds us page after page, that one of the greatest gifts we can give to those who have served is our loving and listening ear. We can receive them to our souls as the treasured persons they are. We can bear witness to their service, hear their remarkable stories, and learn from their wisdom.

In the beginning of my Foreword, I referenced Isaiah 6:8 which is a verse that many who serve keep close to their heart as they face insurmountable darkness. Yet, it is one which could apply to any of us, in that we can also say to God, *"Here am I, send me,"* as we each find ways to support our returning public servants. Many of us have defined missions in life, but to be among those who offer our support to our service wounded is really something for each of to take up with our whole heart because, though many of us were not called ourselves to serve in harm's way, we are nonetheless, called to love.

This beautiful manuscript is all about love, as well as the faith and courage of those who have survived deployment and in some cases, the battle after the battle upon returning home. I have no doubt that "A Leap of Faith" will be a rich source of encouragement for all of us, but I pray that Jenny Lasala's pages will inspire a resolve to seize every opportunity possible to build relationships with our returning Heroes and help them find sure footing on their new path as we reflect back to them how invaluable they are to us today.

For those of you who have paid the price of freedom to include your families, I join with Ms. La Sala in extending my deepest gratitude and may God fill your heart with peace as you come to know how many millions of Americans would be honored to be called your friend.

Ann M. Wolf

Chaplain, Songwriter, Recording Artist, Author

https://www.annwolfmusic.org/

DEDICATION

A LEAP OF FAITH is dedicated to all who bravely served and lost their lives both on the battlefield of war and upon returning home.

"It's been seven years now. This is my brother, Daniel Alexander, pictured on the left who served bravely in the 1st Infantry division of the United States Army. His last name is different because he has a different father. Over the course of two years, he saw many of his friends die. He killed people, as a Soldier is trained to do, and couldn't get over the spiritual and mental effects of that which he had done.

When he came home, he was torn up. He turned to substance abuse to try and cover up his pain. But after a few weeks of civilian life, and time of reflection on the deeds he had done for his country, he decided he couldn't go on living anymore, and committed suicide. I was 11 years old when my father came through the door and told me what my brother had done. He went through two years of duty and combat to come home, and not be able to handle what he had done took his own life.

We used to goof around and have fun all the time, but afterwards when he came home on leave the first time, there was this time where he like went into this kind of mode, where I guess he didn't realize he wasn't in a situation, and I started to wrestle with him, and that was probably a mistake because he put my arm behind my back HARD and it hurt really bad and I started to cry. But he felt really bad afterwards and apologized and hugged me.

He was such a good person. I remember one time, when I was ten years old, he told me that when he was going through a village in Iraq, a kid about my age at the time ran at his squadron with a knife, and they shot him. And Danny told me, that he used to dream almost every night that the kid was me.

I love him so much. I wish every day that I could have him back." ~ James McCormick

Psalm 91:1

Whoever dwells in the shelter of the Most High will rest in the shadow of the Almighty.

INTRODUCTION

A s a child, I have vivid memories of my two cousins playing with their armies of little green army men and creating the sound of explosions and gunfire. They spent hours pretending to be Soldiers. Even at a young age, we glamorized war, and yet we had no clue. The returning Soldiers of wars such as WWII, Korea, the Vietnam War, Bosnia, Desert Storm and the Gulf War rarely spoke of their wartime experiences. They returned to their families and were expected to carry on with their lives as before.

My father, David Tharp served during WWII as a 101st Airborne paratrooper. As a little girl, I asked Dad what Europe was like during the war. His response, "The trees were tall and the grass was green just like here." I replied, "Oh, Dad!" He was avoiding my question. But he answered truthfully. The grass was green, the trees were tall, the sun was shining and the birds were most likely singing just like here. But there wasn't a battleground here at home. No, it was not just like here at home, not until September 11, 2001...

All who serve in the military fulfill an integral aspect of our society, to protect the freedoms that we enjoy today. Everyone performs an assigned function that makes all other aspects work to perfection, somewhat like a wheel working well as long as all cogs are in place. I have found that when a Veteran opens up and tells his or her story, it is both therapeutic and beneficial to them and others who may read it. The goal of this publication is to broaden the awareness of the war experience and to better understand our Soldiers upon their return home. After collecting and featuring hundreds of Veteran stories, they have expressed tremendous healing and a heaviness being lifted from their souls in the process.

First of all, we wish to offer our gratitude and appreciation to all of the men and women who have deployed. The mere words of, "Thank You", does not seem to be enough. We must all take an interest in our mothers, father, sisters, daughters and sons who serve and to be mindful of any changes upon their return. By interviewing and collecting our Veteran's stories, we hope to bridge the gap between military and civilian alike with the realization that we are all connected. Once we understand the needs of our Soldiers as they return home, we can put important steps in place to make their transition back home a smooth one.

For those of you that find it is to difficult to approach a Soldier and say, "Thank You," a hand salute can speak volumes and warm another's heart. When Soldiers return from a deployment, let alone multiple tours, trying to maneuver back into civilian life can be a daunting task. Try to imagine your world for one or more years being filled with daily tasks of search and rescue, conducting raids and capturing assigned targets and then attempting to secure a civilian job with such a high skill set, customized for the military. This is why many returning Soldiers of the past and present find themselves applying for and securing jobs as policemen, bodyguards, firemen or private investigators. All of this is fine, but what we are also hoping to accomplish is the mindset of the civilian employment market place who need to realize that the skills learned in the military are not to be feared but rather a skill set that equals a successful, disciplined team player, organized and multitasking individual, a perfect candidate to receive new training in any field.

When I initially began asking these Soldiers for their favorite psalm, I was fearful that they would reject being a part of this book project due to the spiritual nature. I was pleasantly encouraged, as every Veteran promptly came back with his or her psalm of choice.

For many of those who return from deployment, they suffer accolades of guilt for having survived war atrocities and for surviving themselves when being so close to death's door. Suicides have always existed but are increasing at a dangerously high rate with 22 per day. These are real people dealing with unimaginable pain.

A LEAP OF FAITH is a collection of brotherhood and sisterhood of military Veterans post 9/11, each with their own story to share suffering from PTSD to IED injuries. Each Soldier faced varying hurdles on their journey leading up to the military and transitioning back to civilian life. The women Veterans revealed a special vulnerability undergoing the drastic change and uncomfortable truths about double standards regarding gender in the military. It is our desire that these stories will deepen the understanding of how poorly the military prepares its Soldiers for the high stakes shift from deployment back to civilian life.

The idea for collecting the stories from Iraq and Afghanistan Veterans came to me in a dream. The dream was about my father saying, *"Forget about my war and focus on Soldiers of the now"*. It was after I published my father's wartime letters in the book Comes A Soldier's Whisper. As I interviewed the men and women who served in Iraq, and Afghanistan as well as stateside, they all came back with the same message. And that was after America was attacked on 9/11, they wanted to do something to help and enlisted in the military. It was in that moment that I realized they each took a leap of faith not knowing what was ahead of them. But they knew what they were leaving behind and were intent on protecting it, hence, the book title emerged as A Leap of Faith, The Men and Women Who Served Post 9/11. Their faith also emerged as strength and resonates through their incredible stories. Each Veteran story is preceded by their favorite Psalm.

This has been a spiritual awakening on many levels for me. I hope it will be the same for those who read A Leap of Faith.

ISAIAH 6:8

Also I heard the voice of the Lord,
saying:
"Whom shall I send,
And who will go for Us?
Then I said, "Here am I, send me."

KAROLYN SMITH

U.S. ARMY
IRAQ

"THIS IS A GLOBAL WAR THAT'S
BEEN COMING SINCE 420AD."

My grandfather on my mother's side was a Merchant Marine in WWII.

He passed away in the 90's and never spoke of his experience. My grandfather on my dad's side was a WWII Marine, and passed before I was born. But I read about him in books; he was a full

Bird Colonel in the Marine Corps. Dad was a Vietnam Army Veteran, and despite little snippets of his time in Vietnam, there was not much discussion about service.

Prior to enlisting, I was a Velodrome Sprinter and attempting an Olympic level achievement. My first big race was in 1989 at the US Olympic Festival in Norman. We were the "hopefuls" in our respective sports and marched in the Opening Ceremonies with Ronald Reagan as the guest speaker!

I moved to Sydney Australia in 1994 to train at the Australian Institute of Sport. When I came home, I set my sights on the Sydney Olympics but I had a few minor injuries and then 9/11 came… When I went to the Army recruiter in San Diego, I was in the best shape of my life coming off my season. I told them that I wanted a non-typical job for women, to be stationed in Europe and to go to a rapid deployment unit. That's exactly what I got. As an "MP" I had all types of cases that normal civilian law enforcement had (car chases, arrests, murder, suicide, theft etc. etc.). When I deployed I had 4 job duties, conducting combat patrols within the NW sector of Baghdad, conduct raids on suspected terrorist home, teach over 200 Iraqi police officers how to conduct law enforcement operations and Personal Security Detachment (PSD), a high threat position that enabled us to transport a high risk target and get them to a safe place.

From April 2002 to December 2005 I was with the 127th Military Police Company (709th MP Battalion, 18th MP Brigade, 5th Corps, Hanau, Germany) and from 2007 to 2014 I served with the 382nd MP Detachment in San Diego (Reserves). I have over 300 Combat patrols in one of the most difficult sectors in Iraq. I was engaged daily with small arms fire, improvised explosive devices (IED) and car bombs (VBIED). I was awarded the Army Commendation Medal for Exceptional Meritorious Service. I was also awarded the Combat Action Badge for "directly engaging the enemy". On Sept 7, 2004, I was standing next to Lt. Tim Price, who would be shot in the face and killed, and died at my feet. Lt. Tim Price's death was a defining moment for me. When Lt. Tim price was killed it was a day that shattered the sense of security he brought to our team. As I leaned down to help him and discovered he was dead, I realized that I was in perfect line of sight of the shooter. It wasn't more than a few seconds when I asked out loud, "Just go ahead and do it man, get it over with," and found myself getting mad at the shooter for making me wait too long to kill me. I don't know why he didn't kill me. It was the most vulnerable moment of my life, completely stripped bare and waiting to die. I felt like I was the only one on the entire planet for that moment. What struck me most was the gunner that I drove that day. As I looked at him to provide cover fire, he froze from the sight.

In the Al Shula Providence of Baghdad, we quelled an attack by over 80 well-armed insurgents (see ARCOM) and cleared the area of their presence. We permanently removed them from the Earth. For the first 6 months we were engaged daily with a very active and brutal sector to patrol. I had 8 Iraqi Police stations to train and show them what I did with what they had. That was our soul mission, but as the war progressed, we found we had to start conducting Raids, for which I was placed 2nd in the stack and would dynamically enter a home to capture wanted individuals. I think being a turret gunner as a woman stripped me of my gender (not in a bad way) and allowed me to become the very best of who I am, find all my strength and to persevere within chaos. The feelings and emotions had to be completely contained, until I got home, for if you had a bad day at this job, you were not coming home.

After coming home my brain wanted to process Iraq and the endless movie reel in my head. As long as my eyes were open the movie was playing, over and over again. It made me easily agitated, angry and scared. I called off a wedding with no way to explain to my fiancée what was going on. There was no avenue to articulate my issues even though he was a Veteran with the Australian Army. I think combat is harder emotionally on women, and while I will always encourage women to serve and move forward with deployments, I could have benefitted from a group of women like me. I was linked with the WWP, but they put me in a sexual assault group. They said, "well, we don't have any other combat Veteran females, so this is the best we have". I decided to go to the VA PTSD clinic and that pretty much saved me. I stayed single for a very long time but recently found a Veteran who likes me the way I am.

The worst part was seeing how the jihadists murdered children and grandmas and grandpa's just to get to me. It was their own people and they didn't care. It was difficult watching women who would never be anything in this lifetime because they were born to that culture. I sometimes wonder if my inspiring them made their life that much worse to know, had they been born anywhere else, they maybe could of made a better life.

I suffered some injuries and have a herniated L4 L5s1 and secondary to inhalation from inhaling a bomb blast. There was one too many bomb blasts that knocked me out for a couple of seconds. I have hearing loss in my right ear and ringing in the other and sinus issues from something in the soil.

The VA Environmental Services department checked me, because there were WMDs in our two areas of Taji and Yarmouk. They would use old warheads to create the IED's with Mustard or Sarin gas. I had the vernacular of a Sailor, harsh and full of expletives. You would be amazed at the anatomically impossible string of words you can put together when someone's trying to kill you. I became isolated and lost friends who didn't understand why I couldn't come to their BBQ. As much as the war helped shaped me, it was actually an amazing and horrific experience. It let me know, that when everything is going wrong, when the worst is at my feet, I won't crumble or falter.

I do not regret my service and in fact, I was the best of me in war. I was the best I will ever be. I saved a life and took a life. I was placed in situations of engaging the enemy and except for the 13 roadside bombs they hit me with, despite taking my best friend, and throwing everything they did at me, I would go again.

We had a foothold in Iraq and were making headway. There was so much corruption that we had to weed out the bad, build their force back up, then train them. Within the year, we were getting a few police stations to a point where we felt they may be able to fend off an attack. We have bases in Germany and Korea and still needed to stay for stability. When Obama announced an exit date, my heart broke. When you tell an enemy you are leaving, they sit back and watch. Obama was touting how attacks had decreased. Of course they did, why waste their bullets and rockets and men, when they just had to sit back and watch us go? Two weeks after the withdrawal in Iraq, the Taji police Station and one of my Police Stations fell to enemy hands. I patrolled with those Iraqi men, shared stories about their kids and their hearts for a Free Iraq and I knew they had to be dead. War fighters were taken from the American people in the war seemingly all for a campaign promise. The cut back on the military shows how little the Caliphate is taken seriously. This is a global war that's been coming since 420AD. President Obama wanting a unified globe is trying to strip our nation of its identity and now that he sent folks back into Iraq, we've had our first causality. I feel his hate and discontent for the military people and in 2014, I didn't want to serve under him any longer and got out.

When I came back to San Diego my parents were at the airport. I was welcomed home like I came back from Kansas. I don't know what I expected upon returning home, but whatever it was, it wasn't there. I felt no pride from them that their daughter went to war. My mom asked me once, "Are you ever going to go back to being you again?" I said, "No this is the new me". Once I was in a store with my mom and she turned to me in the crowded isle and said, "Have you ever killed anyone?" and I said "um, yes," and she just started bawling. What did they think I did over there? They cannot conceptualize what I did so they pretend it didn't happen.

To help bridge the gap of understanding between civilians and our Veterans, I would recommend holding a town hall meeting and asking us to come and speak. That way, you will know what we need and we will help you connect to us better. We Veterans don't want you to understand us, but to accept who we are now, and stop looking for the old person. We like who we are. We were tested to our limits and survived. The big issue is for families to get used to the new us.

After I left Active Army, I went into the amazing World of private Contracting. Not many women were on my team back in 2006 and for the next 5 plus years I found that I was the only woman, which made it another long stretch of breaking glass ceilings; I was never trying to do that, I simply wanted to work with exceptional people and that mostly meant retired military guys.

I am 2014 Veteran of the Year for the 71st District of San Diego, selected by Congressman Duncan Hunter and chosen by Assemblyman Brian J. Jones. I invest over 60 hours a year of volunteer time with organizations like the Veterans Village of San Diego and Team Red White and blue. I adopted a very special kitten. Her name is Sophia. She is an amputee and I partnered up with Fablab San Diego and we created the first 3D printed prosthetic and completed prototype. The intent with the prosthetic is to have Sophia be a therapy cat for wounded Veterans at Balboa hospital as well as a therapy kitten for kids with amputees and/or fighting diseases such as bone cancer.

I just completed my first authored book "Sophia the Bionic Cat". The goal is to show what grit; determination and perseverance will do for anyone, through a cute little kitten. Kittens, unlike dogs, when they purr release Oxytocin, it's a natural mood elevator. If a Veteran with chronic depression can't have a dog for whatever reason or even a civilian who deals with this issue, I want them to consider a kitten.

As I go through this process of creating prosthetics for my kitten, I am also opening the door for prosthetics for retired War Dogs and even expanding the conversation into a more advanced prosthetic for our wounded War fighters.

PSALM 91:5

You will not fear any danger by night or an arrow during the day.

Daniel Attilio

U.S. MARINE CORPS
IRAQ AND AFGHANISTAN

"GETTING SHOT AT MADE ME MORE MAD THAN ANYTHING ELSE."

My paternal grandfather served in the US Navy and passed long before I was born.

One uncle served in the US Navy and another uncle in the United States Marine Corps, both during the Vietnam War. My father completed two tours in the Vietnam War with the USAF, one as gunner aboard the AC-47 Spooky gunship and another as tail gunner aboard B-52 Stratofortresses. My wife served in the US Navy as a Corpsman and my youngest brother currently serves in the USAF.

I enlisted with the Marine Corps in July 1992. The United States Marine Corps recruiter was, and still is the greatest salesman on the planet. Initially I wanted to join the USAF, as my first passion is aviation. However, the Marine recruiter said the closest I would get to airplanes would be changing lights on the runway. I wore glasses way back then. My second desire was driving tanks. He said he could get me guaranteed 18xx, the Military Occupational Specialty code for Tank and Amphibian Assault. I heard tank and was hooked, although it didn't work out that way.

Leaving for boot camp, MCRD San Diego was not a big deal for me. The first days of boot camp can only be described as violent chaos, always getting yelled at, having to run here or there and always to slow for those barking orders. Following boot camp and Infantry Combat Training course I reported to Assault Amphibious School Battalion to complete training, as an Amphibious Assault Vehicle Crewman – an 1833, not quite tanks but in my opinion the best job in the Marine Corps. For three months I trained to be an AAV crewman, with time spent learning how to drive on land, in water, to employ the UpGunned Weapons Station and of course how to maintain that 26-ton monster.

I did a total of six deployments overseas, 1993 to Okinawa with Alpha Company 3D AABN attached to Combat Support Group where we participated in Exercise Cobra Gold in Thailand and spent two or three months at Camp Fuji in mainland Japan. In 1994/5 I deployed Okinawa with Echo Company 3D AABN attached to the renamed Combat Assault Battalion and later attached to Special Purpose Marine Air Ground Task Force Belleau Wood in support of Operation United Shield. We were the last US combat units to leave Somalia. My favorite duty was with the Amphibious Vehicle Test Branch from 1996-1999 where I got to drive the AAV and had the opportunity to rebuild nearly every component on that vehicle with lots of learning that served me well later. I deployed with Alpha Company 3D AABN to Okinawa in 2000 and 2002 and again in 2003 and 2004 with Alpha Company 3D AABN in support of Operation Enduring Freedom and Operation Iraqi Freedom. For the 2003 deployment, I was 1st Section Leader, 1st Platoon in direct support of India Company 3RD Battalion 4TH Marines for the push to Baghdad and in 2004, I was a Platoon Sergeant, Headquarters Platoon on FOB Fallujah. After those deployments I reported to Assault Amphibious School Battalion in 2005 and remained there until retirement in 2012.

The 2004 deployment was even more chaotic since we started by living in FOB Fallujah. If you climbed atop one of the taller cement jersey barriers you could see the town of Fallujah right across MSR Michigan. It was so hot; you could not touch anything left out in the sun after only couple minutes. The vehicles were like ovens that cooked us daily. There were dust storms nearly every day along with mortar and rocket attacks. The getting shot at wasn't the worst thing as it was intermittent. It was the misery of the hot, bright, dusty and barren environment was constant and consistent.

For OIF I, I was with India 3/4, McCoy's Marines and we bounced all over Iraq on the way to Baghdad. We got moved to each engagement within driving distance. There was Basara, Basara International Airport, Al Kut, Anasariya, Adawaniyah and several others on the way to Baghdad. During OIF II we assaulted into the city of Fallujah. At conclusion of that operation we conducted mechanized and later motorized patrols along MSR Mobile and MSR Michigan between Fallujah and Abu Garab.

Getting shot at made me mad more than anything else. I was in a position of leadership; I could not afford to be anything but aggressive when there were Marines under my charge. During the assault into Fallujah my AAV pulled forward of the lines to destroy an enemy position. The location provided better fields of fire so we stayed forward of the lines. Every so often we would pull forward of a building to engage enemy positions, and stayed there all night. I think I shed about five years off my life that night. There were four of us aboard the AAV. The plan was alternate between positions to allow each of us to grab an hour or two of sleep through the night. That didn't happen. The AAV is aluminum and steel and when it cools all that metal starts contracting, making all sorts creaking, screeching, popping and cracking sounds. We stayed up all night peering through the tiny vision blocks looking for enemy activity. I told my crew to keep vigilant, as Hadji will be in his ninja pajamas to crawl all over us. As horrible as friendly casualties are in combat, we lost three Marines in OIF I, and five in OIF II from our unit.

The worst part of the OIF II deployment was receiving a Red Cross message. I had returned late in the evening from a patrol along MSRs Michigan and Mobile after couple days without sleep. My CO, XO, 1st Sgt and Company Gunny pulled me aside, to give me the news and hand me the satellite phone. My younger brother had been murdered. There I was in Fallujah and yet my younger brother, the one "safe" at home in Houston was killed. I got emergency leave to head to Houston and attend the funeral. My youngest brother did not deploy and stayed to help the family. There was no way I could leave my Marines in Fallujah. So back to Fallujah I went.

A day or two after returning to FOB Fallujah we suited up and assaulted into Fallujah. There was no time to stew on the misery, it was back to work and there was plenty to keep the mind occupied. But for the rest of that deployment it weighed on me how much worry I caused my parents. The news never portrayed the events in and around Fallujah as anything but horrible, and it was. Although I offered the enemy many opportunities, I was very fortunate and did not suffer any injuries. Of all the moments and experiences, the one that remains the most vivid occurred at the bridge at Az Zafaraniyah. We had pushed into the city and my platoon (1st) was lined up down the main road with second platoon in defensive positions along the river to the left. The Iraqis had blown the bridge so we were stuck and waiting for a pontoon bridge to be constructed. There was a firefight all night long between the Iraqis and us across the river. As we waited in the morning for the bridge to be laid so we could cross the alarm sounded and warned of incoming. A mortar round hit the second platoon's platoon commander's vehicle, Lt. Weatherbee's 3A204. There wasn't an explosive fireball, nor do I remember hearing any type of bang or boom. All that appeared was this tall lick of flame, like a Bic disposable lighter produces if you monkey with the adjustment nut. The center section of the vehicle's plenums fell right in the middle of the road. You could see the blackened troop commander coupala peeled back on 3A204, along with the turret canted in an unnatural position. Then they announced over the radio that there was six more rounds incoming. We buttoned up all the hatches and waited while I sat in my turret just waiting to die. There was nowhere to go and nothing to do but sit helpless and wait to die. The remaining rounds landed on the riverbank and one or two in the river. Medelin and Aviles were killed instantly. Lt. Weatherbee had dismounted to go check on the condition and positions of the rest of his platoon and was killed in an IED blast in his HUMVEE near the end of our OIF II deployment. The AAV absorbed all of the destruction at the cost of two Marines. The pontoon bridge was laid a short time later allowing us to cross and continue the push to Baghdad.

It isn't until things slow down and you arrive home where it's worse and you begin attending the funerals and memorials. There is plenty of time to think about what happened and to think about them. It is not memories of combat, or images of war that are bothersome. It is the memorial programs, seeing headstones and knowing of the loved ones left behind, it is the sound of taps, and the sound of Amazing Grace (especially by bagpipes) that demands greater survival and coping skills. The lasting affect of war has given me an appreciation for the simplest of things. In no way do I regret going, and if offered the opportunity to go again I would not hesitate. I made lots of friends during my service and keep in touch with many of them. I joined the local chapter of the Marine Corps League.

There is an instant level of trust bestowed after meeting a Marine that doesn't occur with any other person or organizational affiliation and is impossible to explain not only of those from 1775 but to the Marines of today.

ISAIAH 43:2

When you pass through the waters,
I will be with you;
And when you pass through the rivers,
They will not sweep over you.
When you walk through the fire,
You will not be burned;
The flames will not set you ablaze.

PRIVATE FIRST CLASS JORDAN BARICHELLO WALBURN

U.S. ARMY

"FATE HAD OTHER PLANS FOR ME"

I served in the Army as Private First Class 1/1 501st. Ammunition Specialist.

My grandpa, two uncles, Mom, and Dad served in the Air Force. The only thing I got to hear about was that a plane my dad was on almost went down while in Saudi Arabia. My grandpa fought in the Korean and Vietnam Wars. Both parents were in during Desert Storm.

On 9/11, I was sitting in Mrs. Barton's English class. They announced the attack on the intercom, and then all of the students were grouped into one room watching a screen that showed a news station showing the images of the planes and buildings coming down. At the time, I didn't understand what it meant. When I got home, my parents were still watching and talking about it. I do remember when I saw one of the planes hit the building. I turned toward my teachers and watched their facial expressions. They were concerned and scared, and I knew it was a bad thing. I was eleven years old at the time.

I was working on my associates in geology at the time I decided to join the military. The Air Force didn't seem right for me but the Army did. Maybe it was because I also knew people who had been in the Army and it sounded like my kind of lifestyle. I was a massage therapist before deciding to serve my country.

I served from 2010 to 2012 until I was honorably discharged due to a nerve injury. I was mainly stationed at Ft Bliss and was more like an 88M (truck driver, basically) being state side since civilians took care of the ammo. Ammunition Specialists typically were accountable for various types of ammo. And at times shipping and picking up ammo from mission points or posts. This picture is of me preparing for a mission.

An average day consisted of PT first thing in the morning. After showers, we checked and did maintenance on all of our vehicles. Then we would run "drills" and training methods of what it'd be like to be down range. During the last year of my enlistment, my unit was gearing up to be shipped to Afghanistan. The group picture is of my ammo platoon during a time of goofing around.

My memories consisted of some amazing people I served with, and even those I served with that ended up commuting suicide. I made a promise to myself when I got out to live life to the fullest, and so I have. The main thing I saw while in was PTSD and TBI injuries. But I knew of more major casualties and I always feel sympathetic towards them. All Veterans, regardless of their story and background, I feel a connection with.

SPC Rice made an impact on my life because he was found in his barracks room dead. He hung himself shortly after we got off the phone with him when we tried talking him into coming out with us during our 4 day Memorial Day weekend in 2014. It really shook me to the core. SPC Thomas Rice is pictured here and he deployed to Iraq. One thing that has stayed with me was the last time I saw Rice, and I barely gave him a 2nd glance. I was having a rough day, crying to myself, and out of embarrassment, I pushed him away and barely even looked at him.

The next thing, I knew he was gone. Thomas was known to be a loner but he was definitely one to make people laugh. He looked after people. He was a good friend. There is a time around the anniversary of fellow fallen comrade's deaths that get my mind into a funk where I fight my inner demons more than ever.

At the time they had said that there wouldn't be a memorial service taken place since suicides were deemed "dishonorable" in the eyes of the Army. However, I also heard that they were trying to change that since more discussions were associating the increase in suicides to PTSD. They eventually allowed a memorial service to take place, where I got to shake his dad's hand. They keep adjusting "training" of what signs to see in individuals who show signs of suicidal tendencies. I personally disagreed with their approach because it was like the inside joke says, "death by PowerPoint" constantly talking about suicide, I was always feeling depressed. I personally think that they were creating a negative environment.

My nerve injury occurred when I was working out. I was hitting a punching bag and I believe I hit the bag wrong. They told me that they needed able-bodies to deploy and that I needed to get out so that they could get new recruits to take my spot, so they chaptered me out. The nerve pain continues with me today and I'm in pain daily. It's a more tangible reminder of my service but the VA denied me for compensation due to lack of evidence. I would need to find a really good neurologist to be able to find hard evidence of my injury before the VA will acknowledge my injury. My husband also served as an infantryman, and he helped me gain back my confidence in not letting me feel ashamed for not having deployed before. I signed up wanting to deploy, but fate had other plans for me...

I have always wanted to publish a book, although at the time, I didn't know what the subject matter would be. There was always a pull and connection to the military. I guess it sparked a desire within me to want to inspire people, specifically Veterans and to keep living life to the fullest (like my goal when I got out). I also wanted to be able to open the minds and eyes to civilians of what they may see in Veterans and their actions. I wanted to be able to give more insight to the misunderstanding between the military and civilians.

As I said earlier, fate had other plans for me and so I published my book, Fight, which depicts what life, is like for many combat Veterans when they separate from service and transition back to civilian life and to continue fighting the fight, and not give up. The following is one of my poems from my book of poems, Words Beyond Life.

A Simple Reminder

Picked up my weapon
With a letter in my sleeve.
The picture of a face
I could never forget
Settles next to the letter in my sleeve.

Marched out in the sun,
Walked in the rain,
Laughed with a battle of mine.
All in a day's work
Until I can read that letter again.

Before I go to sleep at night,
I pull out the picture
And tears come to my eyes.

I take out the letter
And read it once more.

Bombs in the distance,
The enemy is getting closer.
The picture and letter
Go back safely in my pocket.
I again pick up my weapon
Because I'm reminded
What I'm fighting for.

PHILIPPIANS 4:13

I can do all things through Christ who strengthens me.

COLONEL (RET) DAVID RABB

U.S. MARINE CORPS AND U.S. ARMY

"I HAD TO SELF DESTRUCT TO SURVIVE."

I went into the Marine Corps as Infantry at age 17.

I was trained to go to war on a Competition Squad, which is considered the best of the Marines in the brigade for 2 years (4 years active 2 years inactive). After that I went to into military intelligence called SCAMP Sensor Control and Management Platoon. This was a specialized until that focused on detecting enemy movement. We would fly in helicopters and drop camouflaged sensors that looked like a tree or bush and we could detect movement within a radius of about 15 miles. This was part of ground warfare in the Vietnam War era in 1976. I went to junior college while in the Marine Corps and got associates degree and graduated college in 1980 and departed the Marine Corps.

I joined the Army Reserves in 1989 and became an officer, 1st Lieutenant. I was licensed in clinical social work. I focused on combat stress of the Soldier and this provided psychiatric triage, training and counseling. I took on leadership schools and evolved to becoming a commander in the Army Reserves. I was a Major and led the team. In 2004, I went to Iraq and this is where all of my training over the years came into play. I had trained for 17 years to go to war. I was a commander of a combat stress company, which deals with grief, loss, psychiatric triage, and bereavement counseling, educating and training the soldiers who suffered this loss. This picture shows my unit, the 785thCombat Stress Company before heading to Iraq in 2004.

In 2014, I went to Afghanistan as a commander of another combat stress company this time as full bird colonel. Typically, one is only asked to command one of these units. The reason why they asked me to deploy and command the second unit is because they didn't have enough people who were highly trained to do this function. When the Soldiers were killed at the Fort Hood incident it had a devastating affect us. At first I declined, but I agreed after speaking with my wife and went back. I knew that I had the experience and that I could be a much-needed mentor and commander to our Soldiers. It was kinetic and traumatic, but I did it. What got me through this, what my motivation was my belief in God and that I was called upon to do this. My decisions and my lead, my duty saved a lot of Soldiers who were in need of combat operation stress. I continued school and got my bachelors degree Illinois State College in criminal justice and went on and got masters degree from university of Chicago with the focus on clinical social work. This became my trade. I worked as a social worker with the VA and have a total of 41 years military experience. I retired from the VA and military in 2017.

My dad was a WWII Veteran of the US Army. His unit was a segregated one. This confused me as a child when looking through his service pictures. I would eventually learn that he served in an all black unit and that is the way it was during that time. This was not strange for him but was for me. He loaded ships with supplies to transport overseas. He was stationed in

Guam, Texas, San Francisco and Oakland and was responsible for restocking supplies in the warehouses and on ships. Dad passed away at the age of 90 in October 2018. My brother, Nate is a peacetime era Veteran and served in the infantry with guard duty in Korea. My uncle also served during WWII and afterward returned to civilian life. Legend has it in my family history that the Klu Klux Klan strapped him to a railroad to intimidate him and he lost his leg. I've since been able to distance myself from this memory, but I'm sure that this had an impact on me as a child. Although we have come a long way since then, we still have a lot of work to do in the area of civil rights and racism.

I wrote a poem, Out of the Ashes based on my experiences in Iraq and Afghanistan to pay tribute to the Soldiers who died during the Fort Hood shooting. I was affected personally because one of the men who died was from my unit. His name was Captain John P. Gaffney. I have honored him several different ways.

OUT OF THE ASHES I COME

Knocked down by the tragic events of this day that forever changed the course
of my life...out of the ashes, I come.

Though scared by the evil and sore from the pain, in spirit, I take one step forward...
out of the ashes, I come
Off centered and confused in the direction I should take, I sometimes wonder if
my faith will keep me afloat...
out of the ashes, I come.

Moved by the loving-kindness that surrounds me, hoping it will soothe the hurt
and anger within me...
out of the ashes, I come.

I come into this new day. How temporal and precious life is.

Any Soldier of any branch who got injured in Iraq or Afghanistan (severely) would go to a trauma center. Some of them were so broken emotionally from loss of limb(s) or cognitively, they would not return to active duty. I was the director and care coordinator of the US Army Western Regional Medical Command and Care Center. When I was working there I got a request from a teacher who gave an assignment to her children, "What is a Veteran?" and she said the kids didn't know what a Veteran was. I was invited to visit the school and talk to the kids. The children drew pictures of what they thought a Veteran was, but they did not know. The boys made pictures of men staggering and bloody. And the girls drew mostly the American flags. The teacher expressed that this was a problem. One girl drew a picture of a woman Veteran in a military uniform and on the other side of it wrote, "A veteran is a person who defends our country and leaves their family over long periods of time." I then decided to write a children's book entitled, From A to Z, What A Veteran Means To Me.

Pasab was a forward operating base in Afghanistan place where we had a mental health team, a psychologist, and two mental health specialists that serviced the brigade. The location was very kinetic. Our 113thMental Fitness, Combat Stress Control unit whose motto was "Mental Fitness, Combat Ready was always ready." Part of leadership is creating leadership. This photo was taken when recognizing MAJ Raul Diaz with a Bronze Star. He was my executive officer (XO) and a clinical psychologist. He saw a lot of combat, he and his team. One day, we broke down and cried together because of all of the stress and deaths we encountered. He is now a team leader at a Vet Center in Florida.

One of the worst incidents was April 4, 2004, a day called Black Sunday when 8 soldiers were killed and approximately 70 were wounded in Iraq. This occurred over the course of a 3-day time frame. We trained as we fought and so it became second nature to step in and do what needed to be done. For example, there was one squad, which consisted of about 12 Soldiers and only one Soldier survived injury. My job was to counsel the survivor. What do you say to someone whose buddies were all either injured or dead?

There is a bronze plaque at the Vietnam Era Wall that describes the 100-yard stare. For me the one single moment that will always stay with me was the Black Sunday attack. I had to debrief the 80 or so that survived it and they all had that stare. They had to report to me and when they came to me they had just survived the ambush. They were spiritually and emotionally 'not there.'

It appeared to me that they were shell-shocked and trying to process what had happened, but they were all frozen.

We responded to them and reached them physically to help them but it was going to take time to reach them on a spiritual and emotional level. This is a photo with Colonel Rogers. She was a psychologist in a combat stress unit. She was deployed multiple times, but decided not to go back to war when my unit got the call again to go down range. She was a great mentor and advisor to me.

My service experience has changed me to where I am a totally different person. After Black Sunday, it changed me in many ways, one of which is the way I respond to death and destruction. I became divorced after a twenty-year marriage and never went back home. I had to self-destruct in order to survive and move forward. It was that or become destroyed altogether. I have injuries to my back, shoulders and knees from carrying the excessive weight of equipment over the years in combat. I had to go to court appealing my case 3 times to the US Army council of colonels, the highest court in the land. I am the first person in the history of the VA and Department of Defense who has been allowed to include the diagnosis of Moral Injury to my medical records. They now acknowledge Moral Injury and include it in the medical record when the person has a legitimate claim.

The one thing that I would ask for people to do when our Soldiers return from war is to listen. Community heals and isolation kills. This has become a favorite saying of mine as it speaks volumes. I have adopted this as my mantra, which is also part of my leadership philosophy. Part of the mission is to create the mission. If you read the Warrior Ethos, you will understand most Soldiers and how we look at the world.

The Warrior Ethos
I will always place the mission first.
I will never accept defeat.
I will never quit.
I will never leave a fallen comrade.

God has blessed me with a beautiful family!

ISAIAH 6:8

Then I heard the vice of the Lord saying,
"Whom shall I send? And who will go for us?
And I said, "Here am I. Send me!"

Colonel (Ret) Dr. Kathy Platoni

U.S. ARMY

"I WOULD DROP EVERYTHING TO DEPLOY FOR A 5TH TIME IN A NY MILLISECOND!"

My father ran away to join the Navy in 1942 or 1943. He was only 17 years old.

He was selected to be a Navy Seal, then referred to as the Scouts and Raiders. He was the first American to cross the Rhine into Germany during the D Day Invasion at Normandy. His photograph appeared on the cover of both Time and Yank magazines. He served undercover as a British Army officer and in both the European and Pacific Theaters as a highly decorated Chief Petty Officer, once or twice demoted for his antics. He rarely spoke about his wartime experiences and like so many others, buried his own trauma under his rage. He died a terrible death from angioimmuniblastic lymphoma, stemming from the radiation exposure during the bombing of Nagasaki. He was only 57 years old. I have spent decades trying to uncover sealed documents concerning his radiation exposure. The military and the VA cover-up of his death, continues to this day.

Both of my Grandfathers served during WWI. My mother's father, Abraham Greenberg, was the Czar's Paymaster and escaped into Poland clinging to the underside of a boxcar during the Russian Revolution. He migrated to Canada and later, to Chicago. He took his own life by throwing himself under a subway on March 8, 1959. This was kept from me until 2013, for reasons that I will never understand. My Italian Grandfather, Angelo Platoni, served in the Italian Army during WWI.

Prior to entering military service, I was a master's level behavior therapist, employed at a psychosocial rehabilitation center in South Miami, Florida. I worked at several different facilities with severely mentally ill adults and juvenile delinquent and emotionally disturbed adolescents, as well as profoundly developmentally disabled adults for several years. I won a Health Professional Scholarship from the US Army, one of three selected in 1979, for completion of my doctoral studies at Nova University School of Professional Psychology (now Nova Southeastern University). I received a direct commission at the rank of 2LT on September 24, 1979.

Upon completion of my doctoral studies, I was promoted to the rank of CPT as I began a Clinical Psychology Internship Program at William Beaumont Army Medical Center in El

Paso, TX. Upon completion of my initial obligation and one additional year after serving as the Post Psychologist at Fort Belvoir, VA, I really missed the challenge, the adventure, and the opportunity to be pushed far past my limits. More than anything, I missed the band of brothers and sisters and the camaraderie that accompanies this, especially in time of war. After 34 years in uniform, I was forcibly retired in 2013 due to the draw down. I still miss it terribly. Although I was recruited by the Ohio Military Reserve/State Defense Forces (this is an unpaid uniformed branch of the Ohio Army National Guard) in 2015 and am now in my 37th year of military service, it's just not the same. I am a Veteran of Operation Desert Storm, Operation Iraqi Freedom and Operation Enduring Freedom (both JTF-GTMO and Afghanistan).

An average day was waiting to die or wishing to. It was a living hell. I prayed that I had the ability to save souls as many hours a day as I could stay awake and to do what was right in the face of a toxic stew of bad leadership. I turned myself inside out to assure that every Soldier in need received everything I could give, regardless of the danger in which I would place myself outside the wire. I derived enormous joys huge from every interaction with every Soldier, knowing all the while that each treatment session or conversation might be the last one for both of us. Heavy combat, firefights, and ambushes were often the order of the day or at the very least, the relentless threat of what was to come in the form of rockets, mortars, RPG's and IED blasts.

I can recall running for cover during the height of the war in the seat of the insurgency in Ramadi, Iraq and seeing the wounded and the bodies being brought in my medevac choppers and praying for lives to be spared and desperately hanging onto hope. There was shock, horror, despair, hopelessness, helplessness and the overwhelming impulse to help other Soldiers from suffering of such massive proportions from their losses and in places where everything was surreal. It was like stepping out of reality, into some alternate place called HELL. This is what horror looks, feels, and smells like. Nothing compares... There are so many people, both civilian and military that impacted my life, too numerous to mention, both in good and terrible ways. I suppose the Fort Hood Massacre impacted my life in the most vile of ways. There is no recovery from witnessing the systematic assassination of American Soldiers on American soil and being completely helpless to stop the shooter or to save the lives of those who had become family.

Below is a picture and display of 660 flags in the front yard of my office in Ohio and placed by Mr. Howard Berry, whose son, SSG Joshua Berry, took his own life in 2013 because of injuries sustained in the Fort Hood Massacre. This remains a national tragedy.

I loved coming home and hated it at the same time. I felt completely isolated and alone. All I wanted to do was to go right back. I still do. Nothing makes sense here. At least in the combat theater, there is value, meaning, and purpose to what we did. When people ask what they can do for returning Soldiers, I tell them to listen to their stories; to their pain and anguish and struggles. Do something for the troops overseas. Give unselfishly and get involved with organizations that support Veterans and offer up more than a check. Take on something larger than yourself and commit to it. Read books and articles published by Service Members and Veterans. Remember: country, not ourselves.

With the legendary Dr. Ray Scurfield, I co-authored and edited Trauma in its Wake, Expanding the Circle of Healing and Healing War Trauma, A Handbook of Creative Approaches. In addition to fulltime private practice, primarily specializing in the treatment of PTSD for Veterans and police officers, I am the Dayton SWAT psychologist and consultant to the Dayton PD Hostage Negotiation Team. This means I train with Dayton SWAT and go along on all the callouts. This appeals very well to my adrenalin addiction. I am also the Editor for Combat Stress E-Magazine and write profusely for various publications about the Fort Hood Massacre, moral injuries, and the psychological injuries inherent in wartime deployments. Visit my website www. drplatoni.com

JOHN 15:13

"Greater love hath no man than this, that a man lay down his life for his friends"

RICHARD CODY BRANCH

U.S. ARMY
AFGHANISTAN

"I WAS HIGHLY MOTIVATED AND PROUD"

I joined the Army after the Marines turned me down for my tattoos, and for the simple reason that I was tired of my life.

I was with the 1-320th Field Artillery Regiment 2d Brigade combat Team, 101st Airborne Division. I was a well-trained rifleman and Field Artillery Tactical Data System Specialist.

I left on September 24, 2008 for Fort Sill Oklahoma. It started out hotter than Hell, and then they froze us to death by the time we left after USUT training (basic and AIT) later in the winter. I took to military life like a flea takes to a dog. I was highly motivated, and proud. I loved the food and it was free! But the barracks life was something else though!

After Fort Sill until early 2009, I went to Fort Campbell Kentucky to join the 320 FAR and then served in Arghandab, Afghanistan 2010 and 2011. There was action every day in Afghanistan from firefights, car and motorcycle bombs, suicide vests, and Taliban accidentally killing themselves, the loss of brothers, the loss of civilians and children, as well as losing our Afghan partners.

It never stopped... I recorded this video showing Taliban IED emplacers stepping on his own bomb https://youtu.be/ o1YbRqVS6Nk. In this group picture, we were preparing a mortar tube for an incoming Taliban attack on combat outpost Stout, named after our fallen comrade. Kyle Stout is from Texarkana, Texas. The men with me are Staff Sergeant Drew Anderson, my great friend and Jason Trevino. Drew is deadly accurate and even fired from his hip.

Our main goal was to keep each other safe. In the following picture are Sgt. Patrick Keith Durham with the farmer's tan, Kyle Stout in the tan t-shirt and A.J. Castro with his arms up high, all were killed in action in the summer fighting season of 2010.

The Soldier in torn pants was my best friend Justin Ryan Junkin. He was a Sgt., and committed suicide and died September 23, 2011 after we came home.

I often felt blank, almost numb and cold. I began to feel a part of me was gone. It was and is, and it will never be the same.

It was very difficult when leadership was fired over dumb stuff and I found myself under the command of strangers. I couldn't trust the same as before. The worst part was the fear that I would get my buddies hurt or killed. I watched as my comrades succeeded in the face of horrible circumstances, lead the way and triumph in the end. We received the Presidential Unit Citation, a coveted award, as well as a letter from my colonel about my service, and requirements to receive Unit Citation.

Funny the things you remember doing, like throwing candy and water to the local kids. It meant a lot to me to help the local kids in our village. I miss their laughter. They were always so grateful and surprised. You don't see that in America much these days. Everyone is so entitled. It's sad.

I can't remember who or how I used to be. I can't remember a thing, only small details, then war, and then coming home with everything different.

The J-dam bomb takes the breath from your chest from a mile away. I suffered a spine injury and concussions. The earth rose into the sky the day we flattened a village, which had become a Taliban stronghold, a virtual factory for bombs that killed and maimed American soldiers.

When people thank me for my service, I am thankful that we are on people's minds. I think of my buddies. I would ask that people today help the homeless, the addicted, and teach the next generation some respect.

I help my buddies with anything they need, from the VA to mental health and back. I'm here for my buddies.

PSALM 91:11

"For he will give his angels orders concerning you, to protect you in all ways."

THULAI VAN MAANEN

DUTCH ARMY
BOSNIA

"HE WAS BURIED WITH MILITARY HONORS"

I feel very honored to meet people who have a passion for history and really feel we owe our Veterans a lot.

I come from a military Dutch family. My grandfather fought the Germans as a company commander in May 1940 until Holland had to surrender. I have lots and lots of letters written in that period and also pictures. My grandfather became one of the founders of the OD (Ordedienst), a big Dutch resistance group existing of former Dutch military personnel. He even became a district commander but unfortunately got betrayed and arrested by the Sicherheid Dienst. But he did not give up and I have the letters he wrote while he was in prison. He found ways to get those letters smuggled out.

My great aunt hid those letters in a can in the woods and dug it up after the war. I'm blessed she is still alive and even more blessed she gave the letters to me. The photograph shows my great aunt standing with the horses. One of the military horses was pregnant and gave birth just days before the Germans came into Holland.

This picture shows me standing on Omaha Beach as Corporal first class and a cadet at the NCO school. I had finished one 6-month tour in Bosnia at that time. I've been in the military for 19 years and retiring from active duty as of May 2018 and will be transitioning to a civil job with the DOD as a Senior Career Advisor for army medical specialists. I am deeply honored to be given a chance to work with these brave men and women on this level.

It has been such a long way to get where I want to be. I lost some great friends on the way and learned a lot of life lessons the hard way. But I can honestly say, there is no better school of life than life in active service.

On September 11, 2001, I remember cleaning my gear. We were in preparation of our upcoming tour to Bosnia when someone entered my room and said I should come and watch the television. People had already gathered as I joined them to watch the events of that day. I told the second in command of our company that it was expected to be a terrorist attack. I could see and feel everyone thinking about our upcoming tour and that it would probably change all our Army careers and everything forever. I felt like we were all the more determined to continue what we were supposed to be doing and what we were trained for.

Eventually, it did change everything with events leading up to Al Qaida, Taliban, and ISIS. It has become the focus of our military work and a part of our daily military living. I lost friends in the fight against terror. I was awarded the Army medal exactly ten years after 9/11 on 9/11/2011. This was very symbolic for me, as no one could have planned this in advance, since the Army medal is awarded based on the amount of days in active service. I was very proud to receive that medal on that exact day!

I have a 12 year-old daughter named Lyahna. Her father, Chris Kakisnia was a Cpl with the Dutch paratroopers, 11th Airmobile Brigade. He served in Bosnia in 2000 (SFOR), Afghanistan (ISAF) 2002, Iraq (SFIR) 2004, and Afghanistan (ISAF) 2009. He did not talk much about his experiences but I could see he suffered from what he had gone through.

I remembering waving goodbye to him in 2004, when he was leaving for Iraq. His body returned but he lost his soul there... His unit got involved in the ambush that was set up by militias of Al Sadr at Ar Rumaytah in August 2004, killing one and wounding 6 of them. One of the things he feared most were the guard duties; sitting on an over watch tower, with a big searchlight, staring into the pitch dark nigh and feeling like a sitting duck. Everyone can see you, but you can't see what is going on in the dark.

When Chris died in 2011, his Iraq buddies attended the military funeral. Hundreds of people attended but the presence of his buddies is something I will never forget. About 8 young and big tough paratrooper men had tears running down their cheeks while saluting his casket. I guess this is what a 'band of brothers' is all about. I am still in touch with them. They don't talk much and some of them say they still struggle daily. Chris was a long distance shooter early in his career but spent the last years in an Airmobile Anti Tank Unit using the GILL weapon system. He died because of an accident while attending NCO school.

Our daughter, Lyahna was only five years old when her father died. The days around his funeral she made two drawings. You can see the devastation as she pictured herself with many tears. But if you look closely, she drew her father in a coffin with a big smile on his face. I am convinced that she felt that he was at peace and relieved from the combat trauma he suffered. She is undergoing EMDR (Eye Movement Desensitization) treatment at the moment because she continues to struggle with her father's death. Her therapist thinks she feels like she needs to carry her loss and grief on her own. It is important for a child to see, hear and feel that they are not alone in this.

She still has a hard time visiting her father's grave. However, she seems to find comfort at an American Soldier's grave in Normandy that we have adopted and to which we travel to visit 3 to 4 times a year. She chose that grave for a bigger reason I think. It's because of her we started our search for any relatives of Cpl Shearer, the grave she seems to bond with at Colleville.

She knows how hard it is to lose someone you love and yet she finds so much comfort in taking care of some of the WW2 graves. It's pretty amazing. I am very proud my daughter feels that way. She always go there to lay flowers. She is getting older now and starting to realize more things now that she is becoming a teenager. The loss of her dad still plays a big part in her life and she struggles coping with her loss. We adopted two graves in Normandy and recently she said, "Mom those two adopted graves, they are like my brothers now right?" I could not be more proud of her.

I decided to give her a very special gift: the name of that paratrooper will be added to the Paratrooper Wall in Normandy reflecting also her father by mention of the slogan of the 507 as well the slogan of her fathers paratrooper unit (11 airmobile). The Plaquette will be revealed in August.

I am dedicated to spending my time on getting things right for those whose voices were silenced while fighting for my country. My daughter's generation is tasked with preserving the soldier's stories in the future.

As a Gold Star child she knows what it is like and I know it will be safe with her!

DEUTERONOMY 31:6

Then Moses went and spoke these words to all Israel.

"Be strong and of good courage, do not fear nor be afraid of them;
For the Lord Your God, He is the One who goes with you.
He will not leave you nor forsake you."

SGT. BRIAN CONWELL

U.S. ARMY (RETIRED)
IRAQ

"I WANTED THEM GONE."

My family has been in every conflict that America has been in.

As a kid, I played in the woods and pretended we were in the Army. It was my dream. I was in the Army ROTC in high school and was the first to make Command Sergeant Major of the school. That is normally a senior's position. I was given a medal of leadership from the governor during 1998 at Brookland Casey High School in Columbia, South Carolina.

Prior to entering the military, I was a commercial plumber in the city of Charlotte, North Carolina. The Army was my choice of enlistment and I went to Warriors Leader courses, Combat Life Savers, Combative Level 3, Hazmat Class for Motor Pools and many more. In addition I went to Barton Community College for my Hazmat degree and my OSHA Safety training course. I was a Generator Mechanic and responsible for powering anything down range. I was excited to leave for Basic. The training was fun and I had a blast learning so much in Fort Knox, Kentucky. We had lots of freedom on the weekends to roam around and explore. I took to the Army like a duck takes to water. This was my dream job. I took all that I could and pushed myself hard. While in Germany, I was the most southern red neck they every saw and my accent was deep. Everyone wanted to hear me talk and nicknamed me, "Big Country." It was also hard to miss my 6'6" frame.

I was in Charlotte, North Carolina for the Reserves in 2007 and 2008 in Graffenver, Germany from 2008 to 2010. We deployed with the 172nd Infantry Brigade February 2010 to June 2011. Our Motor pool worked on generators and nothing else. I was also trained as an NCO with Hazmat, Safety, Fire and OSHA. We got hit with mortars all of the time. It was 145 degrees on average. I was also a gunner. I was amped up 24/7 and would go to the gym to take my mind off of what was going on. I was angry, and I guess that was the best mood to be in while you were on watch and never knowing what was going to happen. As a gunner, you got to see a lot of the country and flying in a Back Hawk, you saw even more. The locals would come on the Fob to pick up trash and you could see the hate in their eyes. It was scary and we had to be ready to fight at all times. This was the toughest part, having to deal with the locals, as it was difficult to tell if they were planning an attack or not. I wanted them gone. I am pictured here with the 240 Bravo Ammo draped around me. We were heading out on convoy that day.

When it was time for my deployment to end, my Soldiers that I led said that I was the best NCO they ever had and that I changed their lives. They wanted to be like me. I have watched some of my old Soldiers grow in great leaders and NCO's. I'm proud of you all and I am honored to have served with you and by you all. It's a wonderful feeling to know there are strong men out there leading the way for others. When I left, I was in the best shape of my life. However my life would be forever changed on January 6, 2014, when I was riding on a Trooper Drive down a hill about 45 MPH and hit black ice, losing control of my car and crashing into a ravine. This crushed both of my legs. I lost the left leg from the knee down and the right leg was saved with 30 screws, 4 pates and a 10-inch rod. I was in the hospital for eleven months and can only walk with the help of crutches at this time. I weight lift to be as strong as I can.

My service experience has left me always being on watch out of habit. I have nightmares from deployment and have been told it is worse for someone like me who put their heart, soul and passion into the fight. It was an honor to serve my country. I am proud of my service and grew up in the process. It was the best time of my life.

I have found love again and God sent me Jamie Miller. I now know what true love is. The trials and hardships with pain and loss was just a warm up and a lesson for what lies ahead.

When I returned home, I would catch myself looking for my weapon all the time. I had a shadow box made with my medals and achievements. My family was very proud and my maternal grandpa, a retired Navy WWII Veteran said he was the proudest he had ever been. He was the one that raised me. The family got together and had a "Welcome Home" party for me. It feels great when people say, "Thank you for your service," and to show their support. It feels great for them to express their gratitude and makes me proud. When Soldiers return home, show them love and never ask how it was over there. Be here and present to help them when they need it.

Today I am the founder and CEO of Branded Warriors Inc. Our website is _BWITATTOOS.ORG_. We help injured Veterans with tattoo therapy. Tattoos give memory and honor to a brother and sister or a special moment from military life. It opens the dialogue for Veterans to talk to one another and that helps release more understanding of what it is like being in war and the survivor's guilt that often follows. There are so many things that can be talked about and stories told through the art of tattooing. The brain releases endorphins when being tattooed with the body going into a happy state. We are adding an out reach program to help our Veterans for just about any situation.

Time is the one thing in life we have no control over. But what we do have is the patience to let the time that's needed to come to us. Make the time count. We only get so much of it so use it well and use it every chance you get. I want fellow Veterans and active military to know that they are not alone. We are your family and here to help any time. Your life is worth everything to your family, your country and us. We have your six.

PSALM 121:2

"Therefore will not we fear,
though the earth be removed,
and though the mountains be
carried into the midst of the sea"

CATHERINE GANLEY

USO

"I HAVE TO BELIEVE THAT DIVINE INTERVENTION, OR MAYBE GUARDIAN ANGELS WERE LOOKING AFTER US."

My paternal grandmother was a U.S. Army WAC during WWII. Both of my grandfathers served during WWII. My father served with the Air National Guard Reserves during Vietnam, and my stepfathers is a retired USAF, Lt. Col., Vietnam Veteran, and ex-POW. My brother recently retired from over 21 years of service as a USMC officer with multiple deployments to Iraq and Afghanistan.

My "military service" was a little different. I began volunteering with the USO at NAS Pensacola in 2009, on the advice of a friend who also volunteered with the USO in Northwest Florida. I absolutely loved my USO volunteer experience and when I lost my job to downsizing and restructuring, I decided it was time for a new adventure. I contacted USO headquarters, and immediately began the interview process for a Duty Manager position in Kuwait. This picture is of me bringing door-to-door delivery of USO goodies to American service members on a remote COP in western Afghanistan in the fall of 2012.

Before deploying to Southwest Asia with the USO, as a paid staff member, I had worked in the non-profit sector as a fundraiser and event planner (1998-2010). I spent seven months at USO Camp Virginia, Kuwait (July 2010-February 2011), in support of Operation Iraqi Freedom (OIF) and three years in support of Operation Enduring Freedom (OEF). I transferred to USO Bagram, Afghanistan, in March 2011 (NE Afghanistan, RC East), where I worked for 17 months. In July 2012, I moved to USO Shindand (Western Afghanistan, near the border of Iran, RC West), where I stayed on for another 18 months. In total, I worked for the USO in Afghanistan for three years in support of OEF. The picture shows American forces taking a break outside USO Shindand facilities during the summer of 2012.

The start of my new adventure landed me in Kuwait City, where I spent the night in a nice hotel and ate interesting food at the hotel's restaurant. Six of us had flown over together, three to work in Kuwait, and three heading up to USO locations in Iraq. On our first full day in Kuwait, we all got to experience the "hurry up and wait" of military in-processing, and as it turned out, I was the only one who was issued a CAC (photo ID card) that day. My new boss picked me up later that afternoon, and I was given a quick tour of the FOB, the USO and handed the keys to my own CHU. Little did I know at that moment that I was living in the lap of luxury...

Camp Virginia, Kuwait, was located on the middle of the desert, and the drive out, often required traffic, maybe 1 or 2 vehicles, to stop and wait while a camel herd crossed the road at a casual pace. There were no paved roads on Camp Virginia so most of the time we walked on hard packed dirt roads, or tromped through sand. There was a mini bus that offered to move people around, but most of the time the air conditioner was broken, so it was cooler just to walk. As one might imagine the cuisine offered on an Army FOB in the desert leaves much to be desired, but they seemed to always have ice cream on hand. Breakfast wasn't horrible, but if you worked the 4:00 pm-midnight shift, like me, you rarely got to eat it. Mongolian grill night was the most popular dinner of the month, probably because we could actually have some choice in what was prepared. In the first 3 months of my overseas experience, I lost 20 pounds without any effort.

USO facilities in Afghanistan, Kuwait, and Iraq (I did not work in Iraq) provided free telephone and Internet access, TV lounge areas, movie theaters, and group activities to relieve stress. USO Duty Managers are responsible for the day-to-day operations of USO morale facilities in forward deployed areas. We were tasked with developing a monthly calendar of fun events for deployed military personnel to participate in during their down time. My favorite thing to do for our guests, was making comfort foods on Sundays, things like: homemade pizzas, pancakes, cupcakes, frozen coffees, or chips and seven-layer dip. This was quite a challenge, given that I had no kitchen facilities, and had to find online grocers willing to ship to an APO address. I also loved our "United Through Reading" program which allowed deployed service members to record themselves reading books to their children back home, and of course receiving photos from back home of little ones, in pajamas, watching Mom or Dad reading a bedtime story to them on the TV. Additionally, we recruited trained and managed volunteers, usually military personnel, who wanted to fill their free time in a positive way. Although my service was as a DOD civilian, as USO staff, I lived and worked side-by-side with the military personnel I was there to support. This photo shows me visiting with military personnel from Croatia outside USO Bagram in the spring of 2012.

The images that play over and over for me are the ramp ceremonies, where the flag draped caskets were to fly them home one last time. In August 2011 there was a tragic incident in which 27 Special Forces personnel, 2 Afghans, and a Military Working Dog perished. What had to be over 1,000 military and civilians attended the ramp ceremony, from all International Security Assistance Force ISAF nations. I cannot begin to describe what 30 flag draped caskets look like, nor will I ever forget. I will also never forget the faces of the men who reverently loaded their Special Forces comrades onto two side-by-side C-17s. The anguish on their faces haunts me still.

Whenever I am asked, "weren't you scared all the time?" or "is everyone over scared all the time?", I usually reply that we did not have time to be scared. Every moment of the day was accounted for, and served a purpose. No one allots time and energy into the daily schedule for being scared. And when the bad things happen, such as incoming rockets or mortar attacks, an active shooter on the FOB or attempts to breech the ECP (main gate), all of which I experienced while serving with USO in Afghanistan. Everyone has a responsibility that is deemed appropriate. The mountains that surrounded the FOBs I lived on in Afghanistan had an incredible view on clear days. I have to believe that divine intervention, or maybe guardian angels were looking after us, given the number of close calls we experienced.

I am ever more passionate about the people who have honorably served this great nation. I would ask that civilians put some action behind their words of appreciation; volunteer to work with Veterans or charities outside the Veterans Administration, such as giving to charities that are helping Veterans in their communities, in particular, those which provide mental health counseling.

I have recently completed a master's degree in clinical mental health counseling and am working to obtain my Licensed Mental Health Counselor credentials. While in graduate school, I had the wonderful opportunity to intern with a local non-profit in Tampa, Florida, that provides free counseling services for Veterans. I have also volunteered with Project Sanctuary, a non-profit organization out of Granby, Colorado since 2015 that hosts therapeutic retreats for military, Veterans and their families all over the United States.

USO Afghanistan, USO SW Asia, was the best job I've ever had, and despite the bad days, it was the most fun at work I've ever had. If I have the opportunity to go back to a war zone, working in a mental health counseling capacity, I would jump at it but limit my deployed time to a maximum of 9-12 months. Despite the difficulties I experienced with reintegration, I have absolutely no regrets about voluntarily deploying to a war zone.

PSALM 91: 1-2

Safety of Abiding in the Presence
of God
He who dwells in the secret place of
the Most High
Shall abide under the shadow of the
Almighty

I will say of the Lord, "He is my
refuge and my fortress;
My God, in Him I will trust.

DOUGLAS SZCZEPANSKI, JR.

U.S. ARMY
IRAQ

*"THE ONLY REASON I AM ALIVE
IS BECAUSE OF JESUS."*

My name is Douglas Szczepanski, Jr., and I am a medically retired SGT with the U.S. Army and Michigan Army National Guard.

My job and specialty training was 13M (MLRS) Rockets-Field Artillery Crewmember and Combat 31B Military Police Gunner.

I began my service in March of 2001, when I joined the Army as a 13M (MLRS) Field Artillery Crew member. I shot large rockets capable of destroying enemy armor, artillery and vehicles. I joined a few months short of the devastating 9/11 attacks. In fact, I was supposed to be on my way to basic training the day the attacks happened. My boot camp was cut short a week because of it. After basic training and Field Artillery AIT (Advanced Individual Training), my duty station was the B Battery 1-182 FA (MLRS), a National Guard armory in my hometown of Bay City, MI. I served as a citizen-soldier for almost 3 years, performing the tasks of a 13M (MLRS) gunner, which include, maintenance, fire missions and unit drill. In 2004 after many months of meeting, where we were in the dark about our future, my unit the 1/182 FA Battalion was re-formed into one smaller unit in order to fulfill a security mission in Bagdad, Iraq.

Our unit designation fluctuated, but it was most commonly known as C 182 SECFOR (Security Force) or C182 MP (Military Police.) We were sent to Ft. Dix, N.J. for mobilization training in preparation for our mission to Iraq, in support of Operation Iraqi Freedom 3 (OIF III). This lasted for about three or so months and in January of 2005, my unit was deployed to the sandbox.

I was asked to become my commander's gunner and personal security detachment and since I didn't really have a choice I said yes. My commander was and is a great guy. C182 was tasked with training over 27 Iraqi police stations, route patrol, detainee operations and Iraqi police academy training. My team leader SGT Vic and I had the primary duty and responsibility for keeping my commander safe; doing route patrol, make sure the convoy was safe and being his personal security. In this capacity I performed over 8000 miles of route patrol and security as an MP 50cal gunner.

My life was completely upended on September 15, 2005. While on route patrol, in pursuit of Taco Bell at Camp Taji (The official mission was to meet the incoming unit's commander), I was wounded in combat. As we traveled from our base, Camp Rusty, in southeast Baghdad, I began to look for threats. I noticed a gray Opel, a German car found in abundance in Iraq. I knew it was a threat and prayed and asked the Lord for peace, protection and courage. Going 60 miles an hour a car neared on the right side of our HUMMVEE. I yelled and waved it off. Then I turned and the gray Opel was there and I started to draw down and began firing and that's when it exploded, a suicide car bomber with 7 155 rounds detonated inches from my face. I began to go into shock and was transported into surgery and almost died many times on my way back home to the states. I then spent almost a year and half a Ft. Sam Houston, at Brooke Army Medical Center where I recovered from a TBI, blindness in my left eye, 1st, 2nd, and 3rd degree burns, broken wrist, face and hand bones. I have two metal plates holding my jaw together, no vision in my left eye and a piece of shrapnel in my brain to this day. I medically retired in December of 2006. The only reason I'm alive is because of Jesus.

My great grandparents served in the Army during WW2, but I never really knew them. I had cousin that served in the Marines in the 90s, during peacetime, who almost persuaded me to join the USMC. It didn't work. I picked the better branch! That being said, I have much love and respect for my fellow brothers and sisters in the USMC. My dad is currently a Michigan State Police officer and his influence on my life is one of the big reasons why I choose to join the military. I wanted to become a police officer like my dad and I wanted to be in the Army since I was little kid, these two reasons together were instrumental in why I joined.

The reasons I enlisted were: I wanted to serve my country, get help to pay for college, to prepare me for the Michigan State

Police and because I had always wanted to be a Soldier. There were a few that bad parts that stood out. Aside from being wounded, which turned out to be a blessing in my life, the worst days were when my unit lost a Soldier, SSG Ricky Kieffer in March of 2005. These events were the hardest to endure. It has changed everything in my life.

My college plans, my goals, my occupation, where I live and my outlook on life has all changed because of my combat experience. I made many sacrifices, as do all of us in the Armed Forces. Due to the loss of vision in my left eye, I couldn't do my job and could no longer be a police officer. I can do more with one of my eyes being blind, than I could've ever done with full sight! If I had not been blown up, countless doors for the message of the gospel would not be open to me, yet here I am able to go and share today in schools, churches and even the government in the military any longer and I was unable to exercise the way I used to. My whole life was changed because of my military service.

My greatest fear was always that I would pull the trigger on someone at the wrong moment or prematurely. I didn't fear losing my life. The return home and reception was overwhelmingly positive. Wounded Warrior Project gave me and my family financial aid, clothing and resources. Fellow Veterans hosted free dinners. Basketball teams gave me free tickets. Baseball players flew us to California for a free game.

Over the years, many people, organizations and fellow veterans have made me feel welcome and given me so much. Now I'm trying to reach out to my fellow Veterans and make sure they are taken care of. I'm medically retired from the U.S. Army, on

VA disability. My wife and I have two boys, Elijah and Micah. I started a non-profit, which I run through my website www. MiracleSoldier.org. I do public speaking, evangelism, preaching and veteran's advocacy. I am also writing a book about my story and seeking to expand veteran's outreach.

I am also a licensed minister and I attend Liberty University School of Divinity online, in the Master of Divinity, in the Theology program.

CORINTHIANS 13:4-7

Though I speak with the tongues of men and of angels, but have not love, I have become sounding brass or a clanging cymbal.

"Love suffers long and is kind; love does not envy; love does not parade itself, in not puffed up; bears all things, believes all things, hopes all things, endures all things."

NICHOLE ALRED

U.S. ARMY
IRAQ

"WE HAD INSURGENTS TRYING
TO BREAK INTO OUR CAMP."

I enlisted with the U.S. Army.

I was a light wheel mechanic with the 26th Forward Support Battalion, 2nd Brigade in Fort Stewart, Ga. Although a light-wheel mechanic, I vary rarely worked on wheeled vehicles. I mostly worked on track vehicles. I attended AIT at Aberdeen Proving Ground.

I didn't know what to expect from Basic Training. Plus, I was leaving my 8-year-old son behind with my sister. Early training was difficult. A few weeks into BCT, another Soldier dropped their weapon on my foot and broke it. I went to "sick call" for it but they said everything was fine. They didn't do x-rays, even though my foot was black/blue and swollen. I re-broke it in AIT taking a PT test. While running, I heard my foot snap. My drill Sergeant was "pacing" me for my PT test because I wasn't a strong runner at that time. He asked what that noise was and I told him my foot had just re-broke. I finished the PT test, (passed it) and then went to sick call, where again, they did nothing but slap a cast on it. I had to have a portion of my metatarsal removed and pins and screws inserted once I got to my permanent duty station.

Once I got to my duty station, PT was challenging because I was the only female in the group I did PT with. I was a bit older than the other female Soldiers in BCT and it made it hard to find a "battle buddy" I could relate to. Most were immature and just unbearable to be around. I deployed to Kuwait in 2002 for a regular 6-month rotation. Once it was time to go home (2003), our replacements came in and my unit moved close to the Iraqi boarder and awaited word if we would go to war or not. I don't think anyone thought we would really go to war, but we did. We moved from the boarder, into Iraq, and started the invasion of Iraq. I also served a second 12-month deployment to Iraq in 2005.

I participated in the Invasion of Iraq and Operation Iraqi Freedom III. There was no "Typical" day in Iraq. We had incoming mortar rounds coming in, multiple times, every day. We had insurgents trying to break into our camp with car bombs and we had Iraqis working on our camp, so we had to be "on guard" at all times. We would have to be in the "motor pool" early. We had to keep all vehicles mission ready, at all times. We would work on vehicles and always be "mission ready" in case someone broke down or their vehicle got disabled outside the wire. Being on an M88A1, we were also responsible for setting up perimeter walls in certain areas. We were responsible for setting up the perimeter walls around the voting polls. I got to be a part of history. January 30th 2005 was the first free voting the Iraqi people had in over a half-century and I was a part of the reason they could do it safely. Communication was non-existent during the invasion of Iraq. My family found out I was in Iraq from watching the news.

During my second tour to Iraq, we did have phones, but the lines were long and most of the time, and I didn't feel like waiting in line for 2 hours for a 10-minute call home. Letters were the best form of communication.

Not all experiences were bad. An Iraqi man once offered to share his hookah pipe, which is a very big honor for a woman Soldier. I was an operator of an M88A1, (very rare for women Soldiers), and little girls would look so wide-eyed at smile, wave and me when we rode by. Being the first woman mechanic in the 3/15 Infantry motor pool and the only woman in the Battalion that was licensed on an M88A1 made me have a sense of pride that was incomparable to anything I have done since.

The worst part was seeing young people die and witnessing the results of IED's (Improvised Explosive Devices). Seeing my fellow Soldiers cleaning out vehicles that was filled with blood and body parts and stuffing them into bags. The one moment that still stays with me was during the invasion of Iraq. We were rolling through this one town and I saw an old Iraqi man walking down the street. He had to be at least 70 years old and had a young man thrown over his should, dead, carrying him down the street. I couldn't help but wonder if that was his grandson or another family member. That was a moment of reality for me. The people were killing became human at that moment. I realized, they too, had families that were going to miss them, the same as the American Soldiers did. My greatest fear was that I would die in Iraq and my sister would have to explain to my son why his Momma didn't come home.

My emotions relating to combat and witnessing the casualties and destruction really didn't have an effect on me at the time. We witness so much death and destruction during deployment but yet; we can't process it right then, because we have a job to do. If we don't stay focused, we could die, or even get our battle buddy killed. So, we come home, are able to relax for the first time in a long time, and then our brains start to process everything at once. So, really, we're NOT able to relax. We are on edge and nervy. I know with me, I didn't understand this; I couldn't understand why I was feeling the way I was feeling, so I thought for sure, no one else would understand it.

Upon my return home, I had an overwhelming feeling that I was going to die and had nightmares and night terrors (2 completely different things). I had night sweats; I was on edge and would get nervous around crowds. My husband and I would even leave grocery carts full of food when the store was crowded. We just couldn't be in crowds. I also disconnected from my family and a lot of friends; including Military friends. When my fear of dying did subside a little, someone broke into my Daddy's home and murdered him; my fear only worsened. After I returned from the invasion of Iraq, I was short-tempered and drank every single day so I wouldn't have to think about it or try to process everything I was feeling.

As a woman, not everyone recognizes you as a Soldier because you don't fit the "look" of a Veteran. I've had people actually step in between my husband and I to thank him for his service while they kept their back to me like I didn't even exist. Going to VA was tough and being called "Mr.", even though my name is Jeannie Nichole. The women's clinic in a huge VA hospital that consisted of a waiting room and an exam room; with the doctors desk being in the exam room was also challenging and further compounded by being made to feel my deployment didn't matter. I have had people tell me that I couldn't be in combat because women were not allowed on the "front lines". This is a complete misconception, especially with no "front lines" existing any more.

Upon my return home, the community was not very welcoming and unless I was in uniform, no one would recognize me as a Soldier. I kind of pushed my family away and there was no way for them to understand what I was going through. I didn't even understand myself; how could I expect them to understand? During my deployments, my menstrual cycle was very sporadic. It took a toll on my body. When I got back, it was worse. I was in the emergency room at least once every month. I ended up having a fully hysterectomy before I was 40 years old. The Army did not recognize this as "service connected" though. I do not receive any disability for it.

I feel it was not justifiable when the U.S. troops were pulled out and military cuts began taking place. I hear people say all the time that they wish we would pull all troops out of Iraq. I have even heard them say they wish we would just bomb the whole country and get rid of it. What they don't understand is that the majority of Iraqi people are good people. They wanted us there, they wanted a change and they wanted a new start for the country and the people of Iraq. The insurgents from other countries were killing most of our Soldiers in Iraq, not the Iraqi people. Also, we invaded their country. We went in and blew up their homes, their schools, their places of worship and their communities; then we leave it for them to rebuild? We went in offering them a new beginning and left them hopeless and helpless.

I feel pride when people thank me for my service. It doesn't happen often, so when it does, I smile and say thank you. If the American people want to show support, I would recommend sending random letters to Soldiers, a card, a handwritten letter or a care package. There are many organizations out there that can provide you with the information needed to do this. Get involved with the community Veterans. Find out what Veteran groups are out there and volunteer.

In 2015, I raised over $13,000 for homeless women Veterans. I was featured in a film at the end of 2016 that focused on the lives of 7 women Veterans and the Ms Veteran America Competition. I placed in the top 10 for the 2015 Ms Veteran America. I raised over $2,000 for my hometown Hero, (an Afghanistan amputee). I have been the guest speaker at my local Disabled American Veterans meeting and also connected with Final Salute INC, a non-profit that helps homeless women Veterans, with http://www.legacy.com "Giving Tuesday" event where they were able to receive over $80,000 in donations.

I am also working on a women Veterans Lake house retreat for 2017 where women Veterans can come, have motivational speakers, learn about benefits and have a chance to connect with other women Veterans.

PSALM 144:1

A song to the Lord Who Preserves and Prospers His People

"Blessed be the LORD my rock, Who trains my hands for war, and my fingers for Battle -"

ARMANDO E. RAMOS

U.S. ARMY
IRAQ

"IT WAS MY LAST COMBAT MISSION OUTSIDE THE WIRE IN IRAQ."

My name is Armando E. Ramos and my friends call me Manny. I was born in Burbank, California during December 1969.

I wanted to enlist immediately after graduating from high school, but my parents wanted me to go to college first. Since I was only 17, their permission was required and they said NO. While in college, I continued my interest and determination in someday joining the military. I was a college student for 4.5 years and close to graduating with a Bachelors Degree. I wanted to become independent of my parents support so I enlisted in the Army.

I became a U.S. Army Medic (MOS 91B/91W/68W). I served from 1992 to 2011 and reached the rank of Sergeant First Class/E-7. My stateside duty stations were Fort Leonard Wood (Basic Training), Fort Sam Houston (AIT), Camp Casey in Korea, Fort Eustis, Fort Lewis, and Fort Bliss, Hanau in Germany, Fort Hood, the MEPS in Charlotte NC, Fort Jackson, then again at Fort Hood, Texas. My overseas service includes a yearlong tour in Korea, a 3-year tour in Germany, and deployments to Saudi Arabia, Haiti, Turkey, Kuwait, and a 1 yearlong combat tour in Iraq. I was medically retired from the Army in 2011. I'm a Disabled Veteran with 100% service-connected disabilities.

Except for a distant cousin who served in Vietnam, I'm the only person in my family to serve in a war zone. He's about 20 years older than me and therefore never talked about his experiences over there. I voluntarily enlisted in the Army in 1992. Since I was a little boy, the military fascinated me. I chose the Army because they let me choose my MOS and offered more duty stations than the other service branches.

My departure was an emotional one for my family. My place in the future was uncertain. My introduction into the Army was life-changing as it is for all new Soldiers. My first week of Basic Training was memorable to say the least. There were long days full of intense PT, cursing Drill Sergeants, little sleep, and absolutely no privacy. I barely had time to think about my situation, much less the life I had left behind me in Los Angeles.

I received combat medical training at Fort Sam Houston. That training included a combination of lecture, hands-on, and practical exercises in both clinical and field environments. The highlight of my AIT was learning how to start an IV intravenous line.

My assimilation into the Army was easy at first, but became more challenging once I reunited with my wife and son. After Basic and AIT, I was stationed in Korea for a year without my family. So after 18 months without them in my life, we naturally became estranged. As expected, they both required a lot of my time and attention. The demands placed on me by the Army allowed little free time to give. The Army had become my world. So it had to be one or the other. I chose the Army and we went our separate ways. We divorced and I remarried in 1987.

I served one year in Iraq from 2005 to 2006. Although I didn't participate in any set-piece battles, I went outside the wire on numerous missions in support of active ground combat operations. These missions put us in danger of enemy attacks and in several instances we received small-arms fire directed at our vehicles. On one such mission, an IED attack on our lead Gun Truck resulted in the injury of 4 Soldiers in my convoy. Rockets and mortars hit our forward operating base (FOB) on many occasions.

The emotions I experienced as a result of combat are with me for a lifetime. I witnessed an IED attack on one of our vehicles that resulted in injuries. The initial moments after the attack were the worst. Not knowing the extent and severity of injuries, loss of communications, and the general chaos that ensued have troubled me for many years. Seeing my comrades hurt is not something I will easily forget.

Most of the good memories involve our meals at the Dining Facility (DFAC). This was the only time of the day where I felt safe and relaxed, surrounded by those whom I trusted the most. The activity inside the DFAC took my mind and worries away from the war going on outside the FOB.

While out on missions, we never knew for sure, if we'd make it from Point A to Point B. The stress and fear is constant. Everything and everyone outside us was suspect. Being in charge, making split-second decisions and actions/reactions last a lifetime. As much as I wanted to lead by example, the responsibilities were heavy and burdensome. I was doing a radio communications check in this picture before rolling out on a convoy escort mission. It was my last combat mission outside the wire in Iraq.

July 1st, 2006 is a day that will stay with me forever. That was the day my convoy was attacked by an IED. It resulted in injuries and the ensuing nightmare that lasted almost 8 hours. The stress from that one event has left me with some deep emotional and mental scars. I still receive counseling and treatment because of it. My service experience has changed me forever. The zeal and enthusiasm I had for soldiering was gone. I also felt like there was nothing more to prove to myself or anyone else. My romance with the Army was over. My career was done. I don't know how else to explain it.

I don't regret going. I'm proud to have served in Iraq alongside my Soldiers. What happened there is another matter. It is unlike anything that exists outside the military. I would die for my Soldiers and they would die for me. That's as high as you can get. My unit returned to Fort Hood in 3 separate flights. All but one of us came back home. 2LT Emily Perez was KIA (killed in action) on 12 Sept. 2006 near Al-Kifl, Iraq while leading a convoy. She was our unit's only combat fatality. I knew her. I often wonder why her and not me…

The reception by my family and community was awesome and bittersweet. It was more than I had expected. I'm glad they appreciate my service and sacrifice. It makes me feel like it was almost worth it.

I was Medically Retired in 2011 and I'm 100% disabled, service-connected. I'm now a stay-at-home Dad holding down the fort and looking after our 2 teenage boys is almost a full-time job. This October my wife and I will celebrate our 18th anniversary. We live near the Catawba River in South Carolina. She's a tough cookie and has stood by me all these years through thick and thin. I'm lucky to have her and our two handsome sons.

I have seen unimaginable poverty, despair, and violence during my years of service. I tried to bring aide and comfort to whenever needed it. Unfortunately, sometimes it was not enough, too little or too late. So I have always sought strength and resolve through my faith in God. My weapon and training that the Army provided me was helpful, but not always enough. I truly believe our Lord God is the reason why I returned home from several dangerous and challenging deployments overseas.

I have always sought strength and resolve through my faith in God. My weapon and training that the Army provided me was helpful, but not always enough. I truly believe our Lord God is the reason why I have returned home from several dangerous and challenging deployments overseas.

He was and still is my Rock.

PSALM 71

In thee, O Lord, do I put my trust: let me never be put to confusion.
² Deliver me in thy righteousness, and cause me to escape: incline thine ear unto me, and save me.

JAMIE HOLMES OLVERA

U.S. ARMY
IRAQ

"THE FLAG REMINDS ME OF THOSE WHO
ARE LAID TO REST UNDERNEATH IT"

I chose the Army because I was interested in being a Military Policeman and my grandfather, mother, father, and uncle all served in the Army.

My grandfather, James T. Ambrose was involved in the Korean War, where he spent two years in Japan. My mother and father, Sally E. and Jeffrey A. Holmes both served. They were active duty and then joined the Pennsylvania National Guard where their unit was put on standby for the Gulf War. They were both on volunteer status but were never called to serve. My uncle, Craig A. Hughes, Ret. Sergeant First Class, served in the Army as a supply clerk and retired as a recruiter. He never had the opportunity to serve overseas.

I had already decided that I wanted to join the military before graduation. At age 18, and after I graduated High School, I left for basic in November of 2003. I spent my last summer working and spending time with family and friends. I entered the Army in November of 2003 as a Private. The departure was good. My uncle took me to the MEPS station in Pittsburgh and I arrived in Missouri on November 3, 2003. I was convinced that the 43rd was basic and didn't think it was half bad. Little did I know it was just an in-processing center, and my life was about to change. Upon arrival the drill sergeants yelled and poked fun but I had the mindset that I wasn't going to give up and I wasn't going to let them see that they bothered me. My philosophy worked and I had no problems. I entered basic and AIT at Fort Leonard Wood, Missouri and I graduated from C Co 787 in 2004.

I was then given orders to report to the 127th Military Police Company in Hanau, Germany. I served as a gunner in Baghdad, Iraq from June 2004 to April 2005 as a PFC. I was responsible for the security of my team and the other trucks in the convoy. I also provided roof top security at the Iraqi Police Stations. While stationed in Germany, I protected the lives and property on Army installations by enforcing military laws and regulations. I also controlled traffic, prevented crime and responded to all emergencies.

I was deployed to Baghdad, Iraq from 2004 to 2005. In Iraq, the air is thick and smells of decay. We worked every day and were exposed to varied forms of threats. My day started with getting up, getting ready, making sure my weapon systems were good to go and getting to the truck where my driver, Hernandez was PMCSing the vehicle prior to mission. This is a picture of my team. Pictured from left to right is SPC Jesse Hernandez (now

SFC), SSG Billy Hood (now Ret SFC), in Baghdad, Iraq. We were getting ready to roll out for mission We would make sure the truck was equipped with water, ice, ammo and other gear needed for the mission that day. Once everyone was ready to go we had a mission briefing that would lay out specific times, places and personnel that were needed to accomplish the mission for that day. We would then mount our vehicles and roll out the gate, where we would lock and load. I was a gunner so I had the privilege of baking in the hot sun with full gear on; I hated it then but miss it now.

Depending on what we needed to do that day we usually rolled to our Iraqi Police Stations. I pulled rooftop security while E5s and above discussed what was on the agenda for the rest of the day. We usually did mounted and un-mounted patrols, random checkpoints, and night patrols. Our primary missions were to train and mentor the Iraqi Police. It was exhausting; you were left dirty, stinky, and tired by the end of the day. We had different patrol shifts and it felt like a relay race for a year. We would come back to the FOB, clear our weapons, fuel up, and clean out the truck and head inside for a cold shower. On our days "off" we were required to service our vehicle, take care of laundering needs, and make any purchases that were needed. This was also the time to catch up on phone calls, mailing letters, or catching up on sleep.

On one particular day, I was on a patrol and sometimes we switched positions to avoid complacency, which ironically does happen sometimes. As you do in a convoy, you often are not only looking ahead of you but behind you to make sure that the trucks are still there and good to go. An IED hit my truck and in a matter of seconds and real time, I came through that massive explosion and kept driving. You never want to stop if you don't have to after an IED. It is a set up for an ambush, so you would take it and make it through if you could while making assessments and getting out of there. It was will and determination that brought me through that herculean dust cloud. I was hit with 4 or 5 IEDs. I lost count. One of those totally devastated our vehicle and messed with my emotions. I was involved in a firefight, where we conducted a Movement to Contact to engage the enemy forces at the Al-Shoula Iraqi

Police Station. I conducted a raid of inspected insurgents looking for gun caches. I was also pulling security for a burning vehicle with US troops inside, where I can still hear the screams and feel the heat of the fire. I lost my LT. Lieutenant Timothy Price on September 7, 2004 from sniper fire. The loss of LT Price will be with me until the day I die. I will never forget our flight to Iraq together, our talks, and pranks pulled on him and his ability to selflessly lead our platoon.

It is something that you never really forget. Pictures, movies, smells, tastes, songs; all remind me of something over there. I remember walking around the Iraqi civilian hospital while trying to identify dead bodies to pictures of inspected insurgents. Some of the bodies had extremities missing, gaping holes in their heads, or just simply unrecognizable. I struggle with those images daily and I still drive as if I'm in a war zone. I don't like people being too close. I cringe going under overpasses, and my road rage is off the charts. I have bursts of anger and take it out on those who love me the most. I don't like talking about it and I don't have a solution.

I struggle with the after effects of war and going through my benefits process right now for the VA. I battle through those issues for my kids, and husband, SSG. John R. Olvera. I thank God for him every day for helping me through some of the scariest times of my life. My greatest fear was that I would lose my spouse, John. He stayed on my mind day in and day out. We would leave notes for each other during conflicted schedules and try to spend as much time together as possible. He was my saving grace. I was discharged from the Army in April 2006 as a Specialist.

I am not the same Jamie as I was in 2003 and actually somewhat better. I am more professional, wise, and grateful. I also lost my patience, understanding, and love for my country. I am patriotic but the flag that waves does not remind me of the great nation in which I live. It reminds me of those who are laid to rest underneath it. I do not regret going and wish that I could go back. Many friendships have formed and are still with me today. Pulling out of Iraq was a slap in the face. Baghdad was a place we probably shouldn't have been at in the first place but we helped those people for no reason. We were pulled out and all of our hard work, loss of lives, and demons that we all have to deal with are all that is to show for it. I think cutting back on our military was a strategic idea and they downsized to save money. I just wish that with the money saved would go to the VA to help support those who fought for this country. I worked my ass off over there for my brothers and sisters in uniform and never once while on patrol did I think of the citizens of the United States. I know that sounds bad, but that is how I honestly feel.

When I returned home the Army community was lined up along the streets waving and holding signs as we came onto post and into the barracks. It was a very proud moment and something I won't forget. My family was happy to see me and since we surprised them, my mom jumped out of her boots when I snuck up on her in the kitchen. She cried and held me tight. I know it was emotional for her while I was over there. Civilians are quick to pass judgment on soldiers who sometimes mess up after retuning back from war. It is a hard adjustment to make and people need to understand that. I would ask them to be more patient and empathetic.

Today I attend college and I'm about to graduate with my bachelors in psychology, associates in criminal justice and human services. I hope to one-day work with returning Soldiers and to organize a group that assists homeless Veterans and help obtain their benefits.

"
Trouble no one about their religion; respect others in their view, and Demand that they respect yours

"

~ War Chief Tecumseh

THOMAS BROVARONE

CAPTAIN, U.S. NAVY (RET.)
IRAQ

"I LIVE A LIFE OF CONSEQUENCE"

My Dad served in the Army during WWII in the European theater as a communications tech in an artillery battalion.

My paternal Uncle John served in the Army in WWII and my maternal Uncle Corrado served in the Army Air Corps in WWII. He was a Bombardier and was one of the 1st bomber crews of the 8th Air Forces in England. He was on mission over

Germany and blew out his eardrum. He spent the rest of the war, teaching bombardiers. Uncle Corrado stayed in the service and when the Air Force stood up as a separate service, he became an Air Force Officer in the field of intelligence. He served in Viet Nam and retired as a Lt. Col. He passed away in the late 90s. *My wife,* Sue was an Army nurse and part of the Army's 8th EVAC Hospital out of Fort Ord, California and spent 8 months in Saudi Arabia during Desert Shield/Desert Storm.

I joined the Navy after college in 1983 and was commissioned as an Ensign in February 1984. I went into the submarine force and my 1st submarine was home ported in Groton CT, USS WHALE (SSN 638). I was fascinated with the sophistication of the propulsion plants and how they made the ships go through the water. My tour in Iraq started on 13 May 2007 and was completed on 9 May 2008. I served at the Gulf Region Division (GRD), US Army Corps of Engineers in Baghdad. My Commanding Officer in Portsmouth made sure I was ready for my tour and the training. He got me practicing at the command's rifle and pistol range several months before I left and I was a very comfortable with both my M9 (9mm pistol) and a M16 rifle.

I didn't go to Iraq with a unit or specific command. I wasn't going to be a combat soldier. I went as an Individual Augmentee (IA). The majority of Department of Defense (DoD) units or commands that went to Iraq were from the U.S Army and U.S Marine Corps. The fight in Iraq (and pretty much Afghanistan) was classified or considered Counterinsurgent Operations or sometimes referred to by the acronym COIN.

Each mission that I took 'outside the wire' (aka out of the Green Zone), there was always the risk of an ambush or IED attack. On every mission, I went out in full body armor and with either my M9 and/or my M4. I had to be prepared to fight back if attacked. A lot of the destruction I witnessed was done long before I got to Iraq. Some was done during the 1st Gulf War, some was done by the lead up to our invasion into Iraq in 2003 and some was done by the lack of management and maintenance procedures and expertise within the Iraqi ministries. They had a fail and replace mentality to the operations of their critical infrastructure. As the person in charge of my sectors and accountable for my team's actions, the worst part was sending people on missions. Thankfully, everyone I sent outside the wire came back OK. Needless to say, I was on pins and needles while they were gone.

The other worst part was the waste of our national treasure, our people and resources. I don't want to make this a debate on national policy or politics in general but we did not have a coherent strategy for our overall mission as well as the GRD reconstruction mission. As an engineer, I hate doing things in an inefficient manner.

My Commanding General was BG Jeff Dorko, one of the best and bravest commanders I ever served with. This picture was taken at the Fallujah Waste Water Treatment plant construction site. A couple of days after this picture, he was wounded in an IED attack. He survived and to this date, I believe he was the most senior military person wounded in Iraq.

This was my Boonie Dog, which was a slang phrase Navy people used on Guam to describe the feral dogs. There was a group of dogs that lived outside what used to be the US Embassy in Baghdad before the start of the 1st Gulf War. A lot of dog lovers in the Green Zone took care of these dogs, fed them and got them medical treatment. Some even made it home under a Program called Operation Baghdad Pups run by the International SPCA (I may have got that name wrong). When I needed some 'pet' therapy, I would sit with these guys on a Friday for an hour, just petting them and giving them doggie treats.

I did witness casualties, but not directly on the battlefield. It was the aftermath, in the Combat Support Hospital that was adjacent to the GRD compound. Wounded soldiers in and around the Baghdad area would be brought to the CSH before getting sent to an Evacuation Hospital were they would be sent back to Germany. In this picture are the two other senior officers that were sector chiefs with me, Army Colonel Mike Moon and Air Force Colonel Tony Foti. Between the 3 of us, we made a bit of a ruckus with some of the senior leadership at GRD. Many of the policies that governed our reconstruction efforts at GRD were ambiguous and we were not shy on pointing that out to senior Defense and State Department personnel. Things got a lot better when BG Dorko took over GRD. These guys were my sounding board, my sanity and just all around good friends. We would talk every night before the next day's missions and meetings and ensured all our people were going to be OK.

Prior to 9/11, a fellow Naval Officer and friend got me to become a blood platelet donor. This type of donation is very different than just donating whole blood. Platelets are needed for chemo patients and for wound care in ERs. I made several donations to the CSH blood bank during my tour and sometime in the mild of the night. I would visit wounded soldiers on Sundays and the 1st time I did it, I was not prepared for what I saw. The CSH does the immediate surgery and wound care to save the life. The patient survives but the site is not pleasant. Amputated limbs are 'raw', bandages are bloody, the cuts and bruised are still fresh. The worst thing for these brave people is that they're alone. Their fellow Soldiers or Marines had to return to the fight. That's why visiting with them was so important.

I remember a young Soldier who was a victim of an IED attack that killed two to the people in his vehicle. He lost one of his legs and had a lot of shrapnel wounds. Sitting in the room with him was the other survivor of the IED attack. She was the turret gunner and she pulled this young man out of the burning HUMVEE and saved his life. Her hands and arms were severely burned. What made this encounter so special is that after these two exceptional people learned that I was in the Navy and drove submarines, it was all they wanted to talk about. I wish I had gotten their names, so that I could check up on them and see how their lives are going.

I had a mild fear of ambush or IED attack while on missions. Our planning was done with operational security so I never worried about something happenings on the way there. When we traveled, it was always very noticeable and the bad guys knew there were only a few places where you had to return. Most of the IED attacks happened on the way back to the Green Zone. On a few occasions, we had to end meetings and visits early because of mounting threats… That was the price of doing business in a war zone.

The Best story about friendships is about one of my Iraqi interpreters. Her name was Shirook and she was Christian. Think about the risk she endured as a member of a minority religion and working for Coalition forces. She was able to qualify for a special translator VISA for her and her family to come to the U.S. and settled in Washington State. In 2012, she called me with concerns about her son wanting to join the US Army. I talked her through her concerns and Bassam joined the Army and went to basic training in Missouri. I attended when Bassam graduated basic training. The whole family, are now US Citizens. Shirook and Bassam came to my retirement ceremony in September 2013.

I will soon be working for an engineering and manufacturing company that specializes in heat exchangers. The company provides these devices to our aircraft carriers and submarines. So I'm going to get back to working on navy ships again. I try to volunteer as much time as I can to a few groups that serve veterans. I'm currently enrolling in a UR visiting nurse program that does hospice care for veterans. I'm also the recording secretary for the Rochester Veterans Business Council. I have continued my Red Cross platelet donations in every place I lived since I 1st donated at the Tripler Army Medical Center in Hawaii. I also used my post 9/11 GI Bill to get my MBA at the Simon Business School, University of Rochester.

I had a sacred charge while serving in the military to lead my people to the best of my ability. I live a life of consequence and my actions matter directly to the welfare of my troops, to my command and to my nation.

I live my life making principled decisions, to operate in the light and to lead from the front.

PSALM 18:2

God the Sovereign Savior

To the Chief Musician. A Psalm of David the servant of the Lord, who spoke to the Lord the words of this song on the day that the Lord delivered him from the hand of all his enemies and from the hand of Saul, And he said:

"The Lord is my rock and my fortress and my deliverer; My God, my strength, in whom I will trust; My shield and the horn of my salvation, my stronghold."

SGT. BRIAN JOSEPH GIBBS

U.S. ARMY (RETIRED)
IRAQ

"MEDICALLY, EMOTIONALLY AND SPIRITUALLY IT CHANGED ME."

My name is Brian Joseph Gibbs.

Our family heritage dates back to a flag bearer in the Civil War. My grandfather served during World War II and my father served during the Vietnam War. They were both marines. I have heard that as a marine my grandfather was fearless and honorable. My father doesn't speak about his service except what I was told before I joined the Army. He showed me how to do drill and ceremony and how to act properly as a Soldier.

I enlisted on August 20, 2000 to serve, to find direction, and to become better than myself. I served with the US Army b 2-12 Cav. 1st Calvary Division, 121st Signal Battalion, 1st Infantry Division, 69th Signal Company and the 11th Signal Brigade with three years spent in Germany, Fort Hood, Texas and Fort Huachuca, Arizona for a total of 9 years after Iraq. My MOS was a Light Wheel Vehicle Mechanic, Cable Installer and Maintainer. I'm on the left in the picture with my best friend and battle buddy, SSG Jamie Whittimore. We served together in Germany and deployed together to Iraq in 2004. My unit deployed to Kuwait in 2007 to 2008.

The emotions that come with combat is something that is hard to express into words. No matter how much training you have, it will never prepare you for loss, disconnect, and the overwhelming feeling of being alone. When I was deployed the first time I spent my entire Military career preparing for combat, preparing to work in conditions that were worse than most and we prepared as a team to combat the enemy no matter what the circumstances.

The feeling of losing a fellow Solider is a feeling you never forget. Whether you are close to them or not, knowing that you served next to them you have that feeling of losing a family member. Going into a combat area doesn't just change it; it creates who you will be for the rest of your life.

I have many great memories of my wartime such as being with my military family, the friends that I made that I still have today, meeting many Iraqis and creating a different look towards Americans. All of these things and working with Iraqi's to help them progress as a country were some of the coolest things I experienced while working within the command center at Camp Danger installing telephones. Just seeing how the big picture works, opened my eyes to what the higher chain of command has to deal with on a daily basis. Wartime affected my look on life and the world. It also affected my look on my military career. For the first time since being a Soldier I finally was doing exactly what I had trained so hard for. It changed my view on life, because I saw first hand how it is taken away in an instance. And it changed my view on the world, because to me it still was small until I entered into a combat zone where people wanted to kill me. I have entire family of combat friends that I know would be there for me no matter what. And not only are those from my deployment, but just the fact I served and deployed I have a larger family of Veterans that are willing to step up and be family at a moment's notice.

While in Iraq I never suffered any injuries, but I do suffer from a condition called Post Thrombotic Syndrome. Since 2004 I have had 6 blood clots and for the rest of my life I will need to take Warfarin (Blood thinner) that keeps my blood thin enough to protect me from clots. This has impacted my life greatly; it is the reason I left the military when I was planning on staying in for 20 years. It has kept me from exercising like I used too. Day to day I am a walking time bomb and never know when the day will come, but I'm still proud to have served my country.

The worst part of the war for me was the unknown of each day. The unit I was with and the fellow soldiers I fought with were my family and I felt safe in their company. It was the unknown of what the next day would hold for us, fearing the next convoy that may take a life, or the next unit that would suffer at the hands of a terrorist. The unknown of war was the worst part that still haunts me today. This picture shows my battle buddy and me in the background and was taken February 11, 2005 while we were waiting for our helicopter ride leaving Camp Danger in Tikrit, Iraq.

Along with military training, my wartime experience changed me completely. I don't think there is any part of me that is the same as it was before I deployed to Iraq. Medically, emotionally, and spiritually it changed me. I found a new peace in life during and after wartime. Life during wartime was stressful and hard, which equipped me with the ability to handle those stresses today. It medically changed me due to the countless disabilities that service has left me with that I still struggle with today. You can't forget wartime if your disabilities remind you of it every day.

Many would answer death. But in no way was this a fear. As a Soldier you prepare yourself for this, knowing that what you are doing is for your country, family and the way of life. The day we lost Shawn Edwards, April 2005 will live with me forever. It has changed my life and outlook on life and is the single most reason I fight for Veterans today. My greatest fear wasn't dying. It was living without the knowledge that I didn't do my best while I was there. As strange as that sounds, the fear of death wasn't there, because I believed that we were there for the right reasons and that we were going to do everything we had to do to survive and come home and complete are mission.

The group photo with the flag was taken during my re-enlistment, also at Camp Danger in Tikrit. We accomplished more than what was asked of us. I was part of the 121st Signal Battalion, and we single handedly installed the largest network ever erected by the Army in 2004.

When we landed we had a homecoming that was mainly for family. Those single Soldiers just were happy to be home and have running water and a warm bed to sleep in. Because I was stationed in Germany readjusting wasn't hard. But the challenge and adjustment was returning to business as usual. During your entire time in the Army you work each day to prepare for combat. As a signal Soldier your goal each day is to prepare for battle. But once you come back what is there to prepare for? We came home, there was a ceremony and we all went back to our barracks and got ourselves ready for the next day. There was no parade or anything spectacular, just a small ceremony and then back to work. After my second deployment there was a big celebration and there was a lot of families there. It was definitely different. When I first started receiving the "Thank You," I would always say, "Your Welcome." There really isn't anything you can really say, but that. But over the years I started to understand more about the sacrifices I made during my service. Most of my 20's were spent in the military and I gave up a lot of my time away from family to being in the military. When I was stationed in Schweinfurt, DE we lost a lot of Soldiers from other units. I went to many funerals and what I say now isn't "Your Welcome." I ask them to thank those that never came back. I say that because my service doesn't deserve a thank you. Those that lost their lives in the service of others deserve the "Thank You." But for the ones who come home, be there for them. Love them. Give them everything because they have given everything so that you can have the life you have. Show them your care, that what they are doing is important, even if you don't agree with the reason they are there, show them you stand behind them, not because of our politicians, Soldiers don't go into combat for them, they do it for you.

I feel that pulling troops out of Iraq the way we did hurt our credibility. It destroyed the hearts and minds of all of the troops that served and fought and just watched it all be taken away. Imagine doing the same thing during World War II and watching Europe be taken back by the Nazi's. We lost countless lives and for what? We didn't fight for land or oil. We fought for the brothers and sisters next to us and to the families back home. Reducing troops is the worst thing any country can do. Not being ready isn't the smartest move our country can make considering all the attacks and the direction our country is heading.

Today I work as an IT Manager for an Aerospace Manufacturing company in Phoenix, Arizona. I also advocate for Veterans and Volunteer for Concerned Veterans for America. I am an advocate to all Veterans that seek help through my website www.brianjosephgibbs.com.

PSALM 23

The Lord is my shepherd; I shall not want.

2 He maketh me to lie down in green pastures: he leadeth me beside the still waters.

3 He restoreth my soul: he leadeth me in the paths of righteousness for his name's sake.

4 Yea, though I walk through the valley of the shadow of death, I will fear no evil: for thou art with me; thy rod and thy staff they comfort me.

5 Thou preparest a table before me in the presence of mine enemies: thou anointest my head with oil; my cup runneth over.

6 Surely goodness and mercy shall follow me all the days of my life: and I will dwell in the house of the Lord forever.

NATASHA THEODOSSIADIS

ROYAL ARMY MEDICAL CORPS
AFGHANISTAN

"I WANTED TO BE A PART OF
SOMETHING BIGGER THAN MYSELF."

My name is Natty.

I am a Reservist Medic. My regiment is the Royal Army Medical Corps (RAMC), I am a qualified as a Combat Medical Technician Class 1 (CMT1), Battlefield Advanced Trauma Life Support (BATLS) trained, attached to the Rifles.

I have served just over 8 years with the Rifles. I deployed in 2011 with 1st Battalion Rifles. My tour of 6 months was with

A Company 2RGR (Royal Gurkha Rifles). I spent 6 months in PB1 Helmand Province. On return I went back to my reserve unit. I have been the Lead Medic for the Coy for the past 8 years. Initially I was the only medic but now there is a team of 4 trained medics with new medics waiting to start their training. I have also been given the task of the Battalions Occupational Health where I teach other medics and the riflemen medical training.

My father served during WW2 on the Suez Canal and Korea. He started out as rifleman and got to the rank of Sgt and then took a commission to become an Officer. He became an Acting Major. My older brother, Simon, joined the Royal Anglians and did 3 tours of Northern Ireland and got to the rank of LCpl during the late 70's to early 80's. My older brother didn't really talk about Northern Ireland, growing up through that time you were constantly worried anyway! It was on the news daily! My younger brother Saul joined the 2nd Battalion the Light Infantry, which is now the 3rd Bn the Rifles. He did 2 tours of Northern Ireland and a 6-month tour of Iraq, 2006 to 2007. He then left and transferred to the Reserve Army. Saul hated Northern Ireland and Iraq completely changed him. He talked about what he had to do to save the lives of his fellow teammates.

My father talked a little bit about WW2. He got seconded to the Para's and I understand he jumped into Arnhem, where he was wounded - shrapnel wound though he walked around with no problem as such. It was years later that when he was having problems with his bowels that they found the shrapnel. I remember his wound and where he had a massive scar across his abdomen, which would ooze periodically. He was also in the SAS, but I don't know what period as his file is sealed. What I remember most is spit and polish your boots, wear your uniform with pride and properly or don't wear it at all!

I have enlisted for 12 years. I wanted to be a part of something bigger than myself and to help those who can't help themselves. We lost so many Soldiers, being pulled out of theatre before the rest of my guys coming home. I guess I have become angrier and slightly tougher on those around me. I firmly believe it's in God's Hands, what will be will be! My experience of Afghan is not bad. It's a beautiful country and I was treated with respect, dignity, and became part of the Gurkha Family. I was sad when I wasn't there to support my guys when Vijay Rai was KIA. It was devastating as well as missing the family and battle buddies I made. WWIII will be in the Middle East. Unfortunately with war comes those who feed off those who can't defend themselves and profiteer, someone will always pay the price.

Highlander Scott McLaren died on 4/07/2011. He was a young soldier who had gone missing and was later found dead. He had been caught by the Taliban and killed and will be forever remembered by family and friends. That was the day when the young man put a side arm to my head and asked me what it felt like… We lost so many young Soldiers on that tour it puts your own life into perspective. Life is so short. My greatest fear was going back to my old unit.

When I returned home, my family was glad I was home safe and sound. My readjusting to civilian life was horrible. I spent most of my time trying to understand why the grenade that landed hadn't killed me or injured the guys I was with on patrol that August! My Mum had a brain hemorrhage while I was deployed and after I was demobilized, it was confirmed that I was pregnant. I was so ashamed; I felt I was the most unprofessional soldier ever. I was 37 years old and in complete denial about my pregnancy. I didn't feel any real connection to what was happening to my body. My mind was still in Afghan. I knew that the guys in my unit would judge me. However I didn't expect to get completely isolated and ostracized by one of the platoons in the coy. People prefer to listen to gossip than find out the truth. It has taken 4 years to kind of get back to where I was.

I am now a mother to a little girl named Freya who is full of energy and mischief. I also cared for my mother who spent 19 months in hospital following complications in Neurosurgery. I resumed my role as lead medic when I came back from ops. As my father would say, don't let the 'Bastards Win' don't you ever give in to them! I am too stubborn and bull headed to a degree – I love this job. It is my passion, calling if you like. I miss my father every day and wish I could still have those conversations with him. I have been given an amazing opportunity to support the BN on an occupational front. What does that mean? Short version is to make sure they get the care when they are injured, vaccinations and signpost them when it is something I can't deal with. Most important it means that I have to develop my communication skills across all rank structures and departments, which can be quite challenging.

I feel I am making a difference and contributing again.

II Timothy 4:7 –

I have fought the Good Fight, I have finished the race, I have kept the faith."

CLARK ANDERSON

U.S. ARMY
IRAQ

"RUNNING OUT OF BLOOD
WAS NOT AN OPTION."

My military service spanned from 1984 to 2006.

In 2004, I worked in a Combat Support Hospital in Baghdad.

The helicopter image shows the landing zone at our hospital. It was a very busy piece of real estate! The other picture shows a little kid that we took care of. He lost his eye when he picked up an unexploded bomblet from a cluster bomb. Cluster bombs are packed with dozens of smaller bomblets. The bomb dispenses them a little above the ground. Each bomblet is packed with ball bearings. They all detonate just above the ground and spray ball bearings in every direction, somewhat like a popcorn popper from Hell. I was told that the bomblets were painted yellow leaving a bright and pretty little packet lying on the ground just waiting for someone to pick it up and boom!

His father who is also pictured with us brought him to us after he developed an abscess in the eye socket. He stayed by his side around the clock. He was getting ready to go home.

We were very busy at that time and went through a lot of units of blood, faster than the Red Cross could resupply us. Obviously, running out of blood was not an option so we would sometimes be called upon to donate a pint. I was awakened early one morning by someone banging on the doors of the building I slept in, calling for people with my blood type to donate. I dragged myself over to the lab, gave a pint, and went back to bed for a couple of hours. My copy of the paperwork got shoved in my cargo pocket, forgotten immediately.

The next day was very busy. There were a lot of casualties and a lot of blood was transfused. I was hanging a unit and going through the checking process with one of our nurses. It was a unit of O Positive, which is my type. I remembered the paperwork I had been given, checked it, and sure enough, the unit of blood I had just hung was mine. I asked the Soldier receiving it how he was doing, and then said, "Listen, after you get this pint of blood, not only will you feel better.... you're going to be smarter, better looking... and your dick is gonna grow 2 inches."

His reaction was predictable...

I told him it was my blood, which really hung him up. He had no idea what to say, which was ok because I had other casualties to take care of. I moved on, and honestly, forgot all about him.

He survived, but a couple days later had to be flown to Germany for further care. I saw him as he was being wheeled to the helipad. He gave me a really dirty look, pointed at his crotch, and yelled at me, "You lied! It's 2 inches SHORTER now!" Then he grinned, shook my hand, and thanked me. I wished him well and helped him into the helicopter.

I have no idea how things turned out for him, but if you meet a really handsome, intelligent Veteran who's hung like a mouse, tell him Doc A says hello...

PSALM 3:6

The Lord Helps His Troubled
People
A Psalm of David when he fled from
Absalom his son.

"But You, O Lord, are a shield
for me,
My glory and the one who lifts up
my head.
I will not be afraid of ten thousands
of people
Who have set themselves against me
all around."

SHAUN DUFFIN

U.S. ARMY, 7TH CAVALRY
BOSNIA AND IRAQ

"A CAVALRY'S CHARGE."

My name is Shaun Duffin. I am from Asheville, North Carolina. I served as a Specialist in the 7th United States Cavalry, Alpha Troop, as an M1 Abrams Tank Driver.

My Grandfather, Lt. Commander W.D. "Bill" Aders, Chaplain Corp. was a Veteran of the Korean and Vietnam War. He served with the U.S. Navy and U.S. Air Force. Sadly he passed away and was buried in August 2016. At the height of his career he presided over the commission of the submarine USS Ohio, the largest in her class. He went on to serve as the first full time US Navy Chaplain during modern nuclear submarine operations. I will forever be grateful for his wisdom and love.

My Grandfather William Aders was a Chaplain in the U.S. Air Force and Navy. He is a Korean War Veteran who acquired the rank Lt. Commander.

My Great Grandfather, William Russell, was a POW survivor after two years of combat during the Civil War. He served with the 6th Alabama Cavalry.

Everyone that I served with in Iraq wanted to be there. It was what we were born for, to fight. I chose the U.S. Army because, while growing up, I always viewed them as the workhorse of our military. I wanted to be way up front, so God gave me the chance.

As a 7th US Cavalryman, I fought in many battles, As Samawah, Al Faysaliyah, An Najaf, The Karbala Gap, Baghdad, Balad, Ad Dujayl and Al Fallujah. Combat was everything I imagined it would be, and more. Coming under fire from a few dozen Russian Heavy Battle Tanks scared me half to death for a minute, and being hunted by insurgents too afraid to show their face was maddening. And the one experience that has always stayed with me is from The Battle of Baghdad, where many civilians died as a result of being purposely put into harms way by Medina Army "officers," their own Damn countrymen.

These same officers commanded vile and desperate attacks on us using blister agents, a chemical weapon that causes the most hellacious fatality ever conceived. As your lungs start to inhale the gaseous venom, they will blister and boil like a lake of fire. It will crawl over you, sticking to your skin, burning and blistering the entirety of your body. You will be unable to scream because blood will be pouring from your mouth. And you will go blind and deaf, and then die after a few short moments.

When they started attacking us much more directly, later on in the war, two of our vehicle's emergency systems registered as having been hit by these deadly weapons. At this stage in the conflict we were all very well prepared for the barrage, as they had already launched many of their heavier rockets at us earlier in the war. Our vehicles NBC System (Nuclear Biological Chemical) is very well made, and protected all the troops in danger. I kill the men that do this to us.

Several years later, the Intelligence community made it perfectly clear why they could not give the media specifics on who, what when and where of Saddam's WMD program. Simply put, the Iraqi nationals handing over the Intel would have been murdered as traitors, on the spot. There was going to be a lot of dead civilian and ex-military over this, because there were just so many people supplying us with information and locations. The United States classifies Intel if there is a truly credible threat of death to certain individuals. And tens of thousands of these deadly toxins have been recovered over the years, hidden away in that vast open desert. Now that enough time has passed, and the threat of retaliation against these individuals has finally subsided, more and more information is being declassified.

My wartime experience in Iraq has made me take words very seriously. During the 2003 Iraq War, the 7th United States Cavalry performed the greatest cavalry charge in human history. We left American soil with 1,241 of this nation's top warriors.

All 1,241 of them returned home alive and well.

PSALM 91:11

Safety of Abiding in the Presence of God

"For he shall give his angels charge over you,
To keep you in all your ways."

MICHAEL WOMACK

U.S. ARMY
IRAQ

"GOD HAS A PLAN FOR MY LIFE."

My Great Uncle Herman Ellis served in Vietnam as a radio operator.

The internal conflicts that he encountered from deploying to Vietnam possibly had a lot to do with him killing himself. He took his own life shortly after returning from Vietnam.

Prior to enlisting in 2005, I wasn't making the best decisions in my life, and everyone around me in my hometown was heading down the wrong path. I had to get away before I ended up doing something that would land me in jail. I needed something that would be a stepping-stone for the life that I am happy to live today. I served in the United States Army from June 30, 2005 to May 27, 2014. When I enlisted right after high school as a 19 Delta Cavalry Scout, I was only eighteen. I joined the army at a time of war and in part to prevent myself from spiraling down the wrong path. Instead of following the un-lawful ways of the streets I sought after the blanket of security that the army provided. The army helped me overcome my shyness by introducing me to new cultures, places, and people and allowed me to meet people that will always be a major part of my life. The Army opened me up and helped me become the man that I am today. My service to our country gave me something to be proud of. I will always know my brothers and sisters in arms as family.

The military is a family, and that is what I loved most about it. You always have someone to your left and right who depends on you, and whom you depend on as well. They eventually become a part of your extended family. I was a 19 Delta Cavalry Scout from 2005 to 2009. As a Cavalry Scout I was responsible for reporting the movement of the enemy, and for being the eyes and ears for my commander. I was a 25 Sierra "Satellite Communications Operator/ Maintainer from 2009 to 2014 and my company and I were responsible for supplying data and voice communications for the FOB/ Forward Operating Base that we were on. An average day in garrison is pretty simple. You just have to be at the right place, at the right time, and in the right uniform. For a combat Soldier there is no such thing as an average day. For a combat Soldier you wake up and take on the unexpected on a daily basis. There is no routine, because if you have a routine, then you are setting yourself up for failure. Terrorist love it whenever Soldiers have routines, because routines make you predictable, and being predictable can get you killed.

My first duty station was at Schofield Barracks, Hawaii with The 25TH Infantry Division. I was there from November of 2005 to April of 2008, and of that time, 14 months of it was spent in Iraq in support of Operation Iraqi Freedom. I was stationed at Fort Knox, Kentucky with the 1ST Squadron, 16TH U.S. Cavalry Regiment from April of 2008 to April of 2009. I was at The Fort Gordon, Georgia U.S. Army Signal School from 2009 - 2010. I was there for training and I had spent that year in holding waiting to get into class, and once I finished schooling I spent a lot of time waiting on my orders after which I was on my way to Fort Stewart, Georgia. Shortly upon my arrival there I was preparing to deploy to Iraq with The 4th Brigade of the 3rd Infantry Division. I had deployed with them to Ramadi Iraq from 2010 to 2011, and in the spring of 2014 I was medically discharged from the military.

As we have seen on television every day the Shiites, and Sunni, are still killing each other in Iraq. They have been doing it for years, and they will continue to do so. During one of these events we were living on a Joint Combat Outpost with the Iraqi Army.

There was an Iraqi Colonel who was working with the U.S. to help provide peace in the region that we were in. His own people had assassinated him on the Iraqi Army Compound with a VBIED/ Vehicle Born Improvised Explosive Device. It had created a lot of chaos, and it was an event that had raised a lot of questions as far as who could be trusted. Many of the people in the country were as crooked as a cane, and it drove us insane. We had one KIA (Killed In Action) throughout my whole unit, and it was a battle buddy of mine who was in my platoon. My squadron had finally captured the people who were responsible for it. There have been plenty of times where I had wished it had been me, but I have come to realize that I have to live my life in a way that would honor him.

The worst part for me was losing a real good battle buddy to an IED. We had a ceremony for him in Iraq. They called his name three times and all three times he didn't answer, that, on top of the playing of the taps, was like a dagger piercing my heart, and an enormous flame scorching my soul. All of my injuries are internal. Anytime you lose a battle buddy it hits you pretty hard, and often times their death is a harder pill to swallow than the death of a relative. My greatest fear was not returning home with every Soldier that we deployed with. CPL Casey P. Zylman was an outstanding individual and Soldier who served with me in my platoon. He was killed in Iraq on May 25, 2007 when the vehicle that he was a gunner for struck an IED (Improvised Explosive Device). He is dearly missed.

In my opinion a country is only as strong as its military. When people thank me for my service, it makes me feel good, and when I'm having a bad day, it helps turn things around for me. One of the greatest things that I've ever done with my life was to serve in our nation's military. It feels good to go places and have someone say "Thank You For Your Service", or "How Are You Doing Today?". Sometimes, all that someone needs is a little reassurance that someone cares.

After both of my deployments and whenever I came home, I was just glad to be back in a place where I felt safe again. The transition from being deployed to coming home was one of the biggest challenges that I've faced, as well as the challenge and transition of stepping back into the civilian world. When I got out of the military I had tried to kill myself on multiple occasions. One of my recommendations to returning Soldiers is to never see the idea of seeking help as a sign of weakness, because it is a sign of strength. I stress to them the importance of developing a plan, and most importantly, sticking to it. I realized that I needed to surround myself around people that were going to help build me up and support me and get rid of those people that were holding me back from any type of progression. I recommend that all Veterans visit www.ebenefits.va.gov and register, because it is the most beneficial way to file a claim with the Veterans Affairs Administration.

Since I have been out I have also met many Veterans who haven't been informed of a program called Combat Related Special Compensation (CRSC) which is available to those that have been awarded a 10% or greater service connected disability or condition from the VA that meets the definition of combat-related as defined by DOD guidance. Disabilities that may be considered combat related include injuries incurred as a direct result of:

- Armed Conflict
- Hazardous Duty
- An Instrumentality of War Simulated War

I now help other Veterans who are going through a tough time, or battling with their own internal wars. I talk to Veterans who are struggling, so that they can have the confidence to get through their own battles. My passion is writing, and it is what keeps me going in life. I believe that every Veteran should find something that they enjoy, and be passionate about such as drawing, painting and displaying your artwork in local galleries, or going on fishing trips with friends and family. I am an author and my passion is writing, and telling people about the books that I've written. It has been these passions of mine that have provided me with my drive in life.

Today I am doing great! This is primarily due to the fact that I have realized that God has a plan for my life. I was baptized in April 2018, and I've rededicated my life to Christ. After four years of separation, God is helping me restore my marriage. Separating from the military wasn't just hard on me, but also my family. I'm going to school to pursue my Bachelor's in English, and doing so has not only been a huge confidence booster, but it's also been very therapeutic for me.

I am now an author of multiple books one of which is FROM A SOLDIER'S PERSPECTIVE and currently writing an inspirational book of poetry.

PSALM 23: 1 – 3

The Lord the Shepherd of his People
A Psalm of David.

"I shall not want.
He makes me to lie down in green
pastures;
He leads me beside the still waters.
E restores my soul;
He leads me in the paths of
righteousness
For his name's sake.

SAMANTHA JEAN JASSO

U.S. ARMY

"I MAY NOT BE WHERE I AM TODAY."

My name is Samantha Jean Jasso, and I am currently an Active Duty Soldier and Medic in Charlie Company, 10 BSB.

I turned 28 while at Basic Training at Fort Jackson in 2012 and recently had my 31st birthday. I have been serving at Fort Drum from July 10, 2012 to present. I have met some of the coolest and most caring people in the military (Veterans too!). It takes courage, sacrifice, and love to say, "I may get wounded, injured, and die, but I am willing to serve my country and willing to help those in need and suffering."

In August of 2007, I graduated Cum Laude from Texas Tech University with a Bachelors Degree in Human Development and Family Studies, which is about enhancing and improving the human condition. After graduating, I worked, went to graduate school for a while, and later went back to working. Joining the Army was never a dream, goal, or back up plan of mine; it was a God appointed opportunity. When I was looking for jobs in mental health (that's how I like to help people), the Army was looking for mental health specialists. I went to my Army Career Center (that no longer exists) and talked to the recruiter about the MOS. It wasn't available and I had to wait a year and I didn't want to. When I decided on "Healthcare Specialist" the recruiter told me we could start the process and if I changed my mind it would be ok. I told him that I would give him an answer the next day.

I prayed that night for peace about joining the Army and afterwards, I believed I was going to be ok (there were times I definitely didn't feel ok, but I have made it this far!). The next day I told my recruiter to start the process. That day my Mom asked me if I was joining and I told her yes. She told me afterward that she believed that was what I was going to do. I enlisted into the United States Army and even though I been through a lot since I joined, I have no regrets. My greatest fears about joining the Army was if I could physically and mentally make it through training and if I had the skills and ability to become an effective Soldier. The picture of me in the dress was taken at the Battalion Ball in June 2014.

I come from a big family and I have other relatives who serve in the military. My Grandpa Jasso got drafted to serve in WWII but did not get deployed as the war was at the end. Uncle Arturo

G Ramos was drafted in 1966 and started at Fort Bliss, then headed to San Antonio. He served in Vietnam as a Combat Medic and left the Army in 1968 as a SGT. He would talk to other Veterans about his experiences and had flashbacks. He died in 2005. My second Cousin Justin Roubidoux served in the U.S. Army September 18, 2008 to August 11, 2011 as a Combat Engineer. He came in as an E-2 and left as an E-4 promotable. He deployed to Iraq in 2009 and went through a lot. He was treated as if nothing was wrong. He spoke about how Soldiers like him battled with the inner demons of war defending our country and just needed someone to talk to. His friend's battle ended up with him taking his own life because no one would hear him out or was there for him.

During May 2001, I was on the roof of one of the Twin Towers; I was with my high school choir on a trip (we got to sing at St. Patrick's Cathedral). On September 11, 2001, I was taking my 2002 Senior Class group picture before school started. I learned that the Twin Towers had been attacked when we got back to class. We stayed at school but had no school that day. I was confused and scared. I knew we were going to war. Ten years after the Twin Towers had been attacked I officially enlisted into the United States Army.

Since 9/11, I am one of the very few who hasn't deployed. I was on the list to back in 2012, but then fewer personnel were needed so I got cut. The hardest part of that for me was some of my battles were hoping that I was deploying with them. I felt sad that I was not going to be right by their side. But I prayed for them. Another hard thing was that I might lose someone I know on deployment. I see the struggles my battle buddies/comrades have after a deployment(s). They stare off into space, shake when they tell their stories, get jumpy or angry. Some of them avoid small spaces, dark places, and/or crowded places. Some of them talk about the dead bodies, battles and comrades they have lost, about not being able to help and save a life (lives), about how they did what they were told, and how they killed who needed to be killed. Many of them sleep little, having nightmares and flashbacks. Many of them cry at night, struggling to heal, connect, and love. Many struggle with guilt, forgiveness, their purpose, and their worth to live.

What if my Grandpa would have deployed? What if my visit at the World Trade Center would have been the day America got attacked? What if life would have gone the way I wanted it to? I may not be where I am at today, and that is to fulfill my purpose, which is this: To help to not leave a comrade behind. I am in my last year of the Army. Some of the Soldiers, who joined and grew up abused, never began the healing process from it, and when they came back from war, their pain and struggles grew heavier.

I can relate to the feelings of sadness, tears, not wanting to do anything, not wanting to be around people, not having energy, not wanting to participate in activities you usually enjoy, knowing you have a purpose but feeling like you are just there, existing, being moody, struggling to think, struggling to function, hoping you don't feel those ways and struggle with those things the next day. Sometimes it feels like you have a blanket of weights on you, being extremely sad, wondering when you will feel good, and feel like yourself again. It's a struggle to stay motivated and keep yourself together at work and during training while feeling and dealing with those things.

In June 2015, with the help from I WAS THERE FILM WORKSHOP, I created a video about ways to bring awareness and help to those in need.

My last day at Fort Drum was March 4, 2016 and my last official day in the Army was March 16, 2016.

MATTHEW 7

Do Not Judge

"Judge not, that you be not judged."

CAPTAIN JOE GEIGER

U.S. ARMY (RETIRED)
AFGHANISTAN

*"I CAN CLOSE MY EYES AND FEEL
THE DRY GRIT IN MY BOOTS, SMELL
THE BURING GARBAGE, AND HEAR
THE RADIO MICS KEY UP."*

I was born in Rochester, New York in November 1987.

Prior to entering service I was studying Mining Engineering at the Colorado School of Mines, working in an underground coalmine and surface copper mine.

My ancestors fought in fought in the Army all the way back to the Revolutionary War and my dad was an artillery officer and went from New Caledonia to Guadalcanal, Bougainville, New Guinea, Fiji, Philippines, and was slated to invade Japan.

The movie "The Thin Red Line" depicted his unit at bloody ridge He had the same job at the same age I did but he was on Guadalcanal and I was in Afghanistan.

I chose the Army, same as my paternal Grandfather, Edwin Geiger. He was an Army- field artillery officer and a Veteran of the Americal Division and every major South Pacific battle in WWII. I attended ROTC at the Colorado School of Mines, then US Army, Field Artillery trained at the Fires Center of Excellence in Fort Sill, Oklahoma. I learned to lead Soldiers, compute firing data, fire cannons; call in artillery and mortar fire and helicopter and air strikes while imbedded with infantry.

Afghanistan is a beautiful country. Tora Boras looked like Colorado but even more magnificent. It used to have trees but they got cut down for firewood following the Soviet invasion. Most days were fairly boring with guard time, foot patrols in the mountains, guarding the perimeter, taking inventory. I was I charge of HQ platoon. We had medics, radio guys, supply, and forward observers, a great group of guys but we were not infantry with the infantry guys even though we went on patrols too. We were extremely fortunate and didn't lose anyone except for minor wounds. But the Afghan army and police got torn up. There was more than once we palletized human remains to ship out for burial, and had to pick up the local governor with trash bags. Paktika was a lot more active since the Haqqani guys were coming over the border there. There were rockets all the time. Our medic blew his brains out with his service pistol one day during a rocket attack, the infantry boys lost one of their squad leaders to enemy bullets, some civilian contractors were blown up, and dozens of our Afghan allies were cut to pieces. I caught a glimpse of some of the most awful things human beings can do to one another.

I hit Afghanistan in July 2011 right at the height of President Obama's surge into the country. My first day in Bagram airfield, we heard that a Chinook full of Seals and Special Forces guys had been shot down and it was the bloodiest day in the conflict. The fire support team my 13Fs and I were replacing had been chewed up too with one KIA, at least one missing leg and the original LT was stateside and wheel chair bound. We had it much easier, and on the biggest operation we did when we shut down COP Comanche and moved to FOB Connelly, our convoy hit two IEDs and found two more. I can close my eyes right now and feel the dry grit in my boots, smell the burning garbage, and hear the radio mics key up. I will never forget how their corpses were yellow in the pictures, or the guys that had been blackened by 500lb bombs that exploded and blew their clothes right off. They were our enemies, and given the opportunity to kill again I would not hesitate. But that does not remove those images forever scorched into one's consciousness.

When we lost Afghan Soldiers, I don't think I cared that much. I will never forget the first hurt human being I saw. It was an Afghan policeman that had been blown out of the back of a ford ranger. His clothes were gone, the back of his head was missing, and his penis was cut clean off. He was alive and the PA and medic were giving him a tracheotomy. I felt completely indifferent, but morbidly curious. He ended up dying, but so did most Afghans that were wounded. One of them drank battery acid to get out of going on patrol since so many of them were dying, and he was puking up blood. He died too. Oddly enough, what hit me the hardest was seeing the destruction of hell I was able to rain down on the enemy. I felt like the machines in terminator. They were barely out of the Stone Age running around in sandals shooting Enfield rifles and shooting 107mm rockets off a pile of rocks. I had GPS guided munitions, aircraft, top-secret technology that I won't discuss, overwhelming firepower and logistical support. We talked to some of the bad guys and they thought we were Russians who had returned. Many had never heard of "Afghanistan" because they lived in "Waziristan."

My wife is a PA and works at the burn unit at Strong. I always say the great things she does every day is to restore karma in the universe by treating burns after I gave the order to burn so many people. My greatest fear is the karma will catch up to me.

I destroyed so many lives and families. But they were trying to fight us and we never killed innocents. But we were on their land. My life is wonderful and full of family and love and all my dreams are all coming true. Could it be this could all be shattered for me one day? Dear God I hope not. That is why it is my mission every single day to make the world around me better, help everyone do everything well, and do everything to atone for my sins. I must leave the world a better place and never forget the awfulness and take my lessons and experiences and use them for whatever good I can inject into my sphere. My life is dedicated to being a positive force to make those I touch, directly and indirectly, better all the time.

I learned that life is so incredibly fragile, and we must be ever so grateful of all our blessings. We can be snuffed out in an instant so live the life worth living every single day. And true faith is forged in the darkness and true thanksgiving is appreciated through hardship. We do not praise God when all is great, and curse Him when all is wrong. There is always goodness present but it is up to us to find the light and not to be blinded in the darkness. I am not a very religious person, but I find these truths to be self-evident. True believing in grace does not hinge on a positive outcome or experience. It is just always there.

I formed friendships while in the service. But I don't keep in touch with them. Partly because I am a busy person and don't make the effort, and partly because they are associated with difficult emotions. My wife is the only one that knows the true Joe.

When I returned home there was no sleep, no intimacy, nightmares, and total apathy. It took therapy, medication, and a strong will to want to get better. It was six months before I was functioning properly and a couple years before I was fully pieced back tougher, but my wife standing beside me got me through it. I do not have PTSD/feelings of guilt, nor does my experience interfere with my life moving forward. Do I find myself drifting back there sometimes? Sure, but everyone has nostalgia from time to time. I am stronger than ever before, happier than ever before, and grateful for my experience. I am strong and better because I wanted to be and now have tremendous perspective on the world that I hope to use to help others.

I have one request of the American people and that is to learn what you can about what we do with an open mind. I was not defending the constitution in Afghanistan, nor was I arguably keeping the country any safer, but I was keeping my soldiers safer just as they were for me. Do not put us on a pedestal. WWII Vets were the greatest generation. Korean vets were forgotten. Vietnam Vets had to suffer. My generation is all volunteers. Most of us are not Heroes and just trying to get ahead with a good job. I am thankful what the Vietnam Vets have done for us to pave the way, but please do not over compensate as it gives an entitlement attitude and we begin to forget the merits of "Selfless Service."

Today I work with local government to help Vets, Veterans advisory committees, and getting involved with the Legion and VFW.

PSALM 32:8

The Joy of Forgiveness
A Psalm of David. A Contemplation.

"I will instruct you and teach you in the way you should go; I will guide you with My eye."

CODY ROBINSON

U.S. ARMY (ACTIVE)
AFGHANISTAN

"I'M TIRED OF SEEING MY BROTHERS AND SISTERS DIE."

My grandfather on my mother's side is the only other part of my family who served in the military. He died long before I was born, when my mother was in her teens. However, he was a Cook during WW2 and spent much of his time on Navy ships providing meals to all of the Soldiers who were en route to fight in the Pacific.

Before entering service, I was attending college at Western Kentucky University. I was a full-time student, and graduated prior to enlisting in the U.S. Army in 2009. I chose the Army based on where a lot of my childhood friends ended up after high school, as well as the kind of job and involvement I wanted in the military. I wanted to be a Medic to help my fellow countrymen and women make it back home safely.

Departure from training came quick, and at the time, I was pretty lost. Coming from college with no real work experience and big camaraderie, I was confused often and passive frequently. The flights from Kentucky to Oklahoma and the following transportation left me yearning for sleep around the clock. Training started very early; so early that the lights on and wakeup shouting from the drill sergeants at 0430 startled me and left me in a daze. The early days of training were very controlled, rigorous, and mentally and physically demanding, as I've never experienced a lifestyle so high-paced. We learned fast and transitioned between topics and training often, as we were in a time of war and we had to be sure we could go out there and fight when the time came. I adapted well after the initial week of culture shock. The physical regiment wasn't too bad, as I participated in the Future Soldier program prior and was in pretty good shape. The barracks life reminded me of college in a sense, but you shared with a lot more people. You also either rose with everyone, or fell together. If one person had his or her barracks locker unsecured, everyone paid. It was frustrating, but built camaraderie. Social life was training, and ensuring we all were competent in skills was paramount. Free time often went from teenage banter to repeating training tasks over and over until we had it down. We were all from different walks of life, and meshed together well. On my first deployment, my platoon and I would goof around as much as possible in between missions to lessen the mental load placed on the high-tempo lifestyle.

I am in the U.S. Army and currently a part of Charlie Company, 10th Brigade Support Battalion, 1st Brigade Combat Team, 10th Mountain Division Light Infantry. I spent most of my time in the service with a part of the 3rd Brigade Combat Team. It has since been deactivated as part of the Army drawdown (and reflagged at Fort Polk to the former 4th Brigade Combat Team). Prior to arriving to 3rd Brigade in winter of 2010, I spent the fall of that year training to become a Medic at Fort Sam Houston, Texas. I gained valuable skills in patient care and management, patient evacuation and treating wounded under fire. Upon arriving at 3rd Brigade in December, I spent the first three months of 2011 training and honing my medical skills with my unit in preparation for my first deployment that would come in April. During all aspects of my training, my job description was essentially the treatment of wounded soldiers and evacuation of them to the next echelon of care.

Fort Drum, NY has been my only duty station. From 20 December 2010 to current (30 June, 2016). The average day when we were in garrison consisted of morning physical training from 0700 to 0830. We showered and ate, and reported to work at 1000 hours. Our normal workday consisted of motor pool maintenance on the vehicles (Monday), medical training (Tuesdays and Thursdays), sergeant's time training (Soldier skills; Wednesdays), and admin/week wrap-up on Friday. In the deployed setting, my first deployment consisted of convoy missions as a large part of each day, as well as sporadic training sessions, where we taught the Afghan Army medical skills. My second deployment, I operated in the command tent coordinating medical evacuation and operating the communications. Daily operations consisted of ensuring the lines of communication throughout the entire complex were solid, and we had a good patient flow and communication system.

On my first deployment we hit a few IEDs, and luckily, they were small and concussions were the only injuries folks suffered. We got rocketed a few times, and the vehicles took some small arms fire from AK-47s, but no actual battles. There were legions of occasions of American and Afghan Soldiers being brought into the trauma bay due to convoy attacks and battles, though. At times I worked in the emergency room at Kandahar's Hospital alongside the Navy. The Navy was very short on Corpsman due to the attrition rate at a base neighboring the Pakistan borders, so they would send requests for other branches to assist when they needed it. In this image and during my second deployment, I am in a sleep tent stretching and preparing for a run around the base. A lot of times, physical training was done on your own time, as schedules were unpredictable and formations of soldiers were unsafe due to potential incoming mortars.

We were rocketed 3-4-5 times a day. FOB Shank was dubbed "rocket city" for that fact. A lot of the time was spent running to concrete bunkers and trying to avoid areas of emphasis that the Taliban focused on us with their rockets and mortars. Initially, panic and indecision about whether or not I could save the person's life. Later it turned to apathy I guess. In a sense, the amount of casualties that came through, whether they lived, or not, deadened my mind in a sense. I cared about the patients, but I was also numb mentally. The worst part was my not knowing if a patient made it out alive after they left our trauma bay. A majority of the patients were Afghan Soldiers, and we had no idea of knowing when they left on the helicopter. I'd say an even worst part was not coming back the same and having difficulty adjusting. The one moment that has always stayed with me was when the first patient came into our bay and our medical table. SPC Preston Dennis was his name. Remembering the PA and the team that was on shift working frantically to stop the bleeding, then the attempts at performing CPR to resuscitate him. He did not make it, and I still remember his face and that moment. In this picture, I am instructing Soldiers who were about to fire their weapons and showing them how many rounds go into each silhouette on the paper target.

The rockets and mortars were terrifying, no doubt. The moment that alarm went off, we booked it. The alarm stays with me to this day, and definitely causes one to jump. After the majority of the deployment, we joked about the incoming shells a lot due to how bad the accuracy was, but despite the jokes, we were all pretty scared. My greatest fear and still is would be to die alone. After deployment, I lost the passive and boyish naivety and became more forthcoming, vocal and honest. I have become more confident within myself and in the way I deal with situations. There are no winners in war. I'm tired of seeing my brothers and sisters die for wars we don't need. I'm all for pulling out. We don't belong in Afghanistan or Iraq.

I'm still active duty at Fort Drum, currently in the medical discharge process for my left knee that I've repeatedly injured to no resolution during my time in the military. After my second deployment, my wife and I continued dating, culminating in me proposing in late 2014. We married in November 2015. Victoria is my rock, and my pillar, through the good and bad.

I enlisted for many reasons, experienced a lifetime's worth of events, and took away enough lessons to fill a library. But the most important thing I've learned was the, in the face of insurmountable odds (and at times, bullshit), the unity of your brothers and sisters are undeniable, and unbreakable. It is a bond that cannot be explained and understood by the outside world or replicated and is one of a kind, truly.

The last six and a half years has taken me on a journey that I will take with me everyday for the rest of my days. From training, to jumping into a unit (3rd Brigade Spartans!) and deploying out the gates, coming back stateside and doing it again and ending it with a company and brigade that has developed me more as a leader than I have ever envisioned.

I retire with my head held high and proud, knowing that I've done everything I've set out to do and hopefully have taught and influenced everyone I've led. I'm a firm believer that if you're not doing something to make someone else's life better, then you're wasting your time, and I hope that those I've soldiered with carry this on.

Psalm 70

Make haste, O God, to deliver me!
Make haste to help me, O Lord!
[2] Let them be ashamed and confounded
Who seek my life;
Let them be [a]turned back and confused
Who desire my hurt.
[3] Let them be turned back because of their shame,
Who say, [b]"Aha, aha!"
[4] Let all those who seek You rejoice and be glad in You;
And let those who love Your salvation say continually,
"Let God be magnified!"
[5] But I *am* poor and needy;
Make haste to me, O God!
You *are* my help and my deliverer;
O Lord, do not delay.

JOSH WEDDELL

AIR NATIONAL GUARD
IRAQ

"I WOULDN'T TRADE THEM
FOR ANYTHING."

My name is Josh Weddell and I am from Selkirk, New York.

I wouldn't trade my military experience for anything. My Grandfather William E. Weddell was a Veteran of WWII. He was part of the United States Army Band and actively played in the band during WWII. Grandfather Richard Bergeron was a Veteran of the Korean War. He was assigned to the United States Navy and attached to a carrier group during the war. He encouraged Josh to join the military.

I enlisted to the join the United States Navy as a Seabee. But due to a foot injury I was unable to proceed with that enlistment and later joined the United States Air Force, New York Air National Guard as a heavy equipment operator.

I chose the Air National Guard due to the great things that I had heard. Most importantly the Air Guard had a great equipment operator's school. The strict and regimented guidelines and the attention to detail led me to become a mature adult. In the Air National Guard I was able to travel throughout the country and become very diverse. I communicated with people from all walks of life.

I am a Veteran of Operation Resolve (9/11) NYC and was deployed for the devastation on 9/11 and spent two months in the ground zero area. I saw things that I prefer not to describe during the 9/11 deployments. The pictures of 9/11 do it no justice. I recall how amazing that so much destruction was done to our country in a matter of minutes and that it was a horrific tragedy.

I am also a Veteran of Operation Enduring Freedom (state side) and backfilled at Bolling Air Force Base, Washington DC, with the 11th Wing. My special training as a Combat Life Saver provided the ability to supply emergency medicine in a critical wartime situation. I am also a graduate of the United States Air Force Non Commissioned Officers Academy and a Veteran of Operation Iraqi Freedom and was deployed for four months to Talil Air Base AKA Ali Air Base. I witnessed destruction and the military changed me because of it. While in Iraq there were numerous rocket attacks. I remember the first night in Iraq and while driving down a road in the base our vehicle started shaking. We thought something had broken on the vehicle. Upon exiting we heard the "Wushing" sound of a rocket and a loud explosion. We were littered with small rocks and debris. It is an event I will never forget.

The worst part for me is living with the aftermath of war for the rest of my life. Although, I am a functioning and contributing member of society, the memories will always stay with me. But those memories have made me who am today and I wouldn't trade them for anything. It feels great when being thanked for my service, but I did my job and protected my country.

I am currently a member of the VFW and work full time as a police officer and now in the publishing phase for my new book, THE THIN BLUE LINE about transitioning from the military to law enforcement.

PSALM 27:1

An Exuberant Declaration of Faith
A Psalm of David

"The Lord is my light and my
salvation;
Whom shall I fear?
The Lord is the strength of my life;
Of whom shall I be afraid?"

ERIC J. PEREZ

U.S. MARINE CORPS
IRAQ

"WE WERE TAKING OUT TERRORIST THAT WERE KILLING CIVILIANS."

I was going to college and working three jobs in one at a candy factory, second as a bus boy, and third lost prevention in Chicago.

My father and uncle served in the Air Force. Uncle Gilbert Perez retired as a Chief warrant officer and flew Apache helicopters with the U.S. Army during Desert Storm. My aunt, Lt. Colonel Debra Perez served in Desert Storm commanding troops. They spoke very little of their experiences.

I wanted the Marines because it was the most rigorous, challenging, and longest boot camp. I was very nervous and did not know what to expect beyond that. I adapted really well to military life and the physical regimen because I was already in shape and trained before I went in. I lived with my aunt and uncle who were in the army a couple times and they showed me how to make a military bed. I saw how they would shine their boots, wear their uniform and iron them.

I served with the U.S. Marines, 3/4 India Company, Infantry, embarkation, Armory of weapons, police Sgt. Who ran barracks and worked along side Gunnery Sgt. Co., Xo, as well as battalion. Rough terrain and night course, tactical small unit leaders course, military operations on urban terrain, military interview/ interrogation, fundamental of Marine Corps Leadership, infantry patrolling, terrorism awareness by correspondent. I was stationed at 29 Palms California with 1st

Marine Division, 7th Marine Regiment with 3/4 India Company. I went to Okinawa, Guam, and Iraq from 2000 to 2004.

When I first was stationed at 29 Palms I got up at 5:30 to go take classes in weapons, tactics, land navigation, but when I started to get more responsibilities and a different role such as Police Sgt., Armor, safety NCO, Hazmat NCO, and embarkation NCO. Duties would be from opening up at 0300 to hand out weapons for rang or the field to getting Humvee to pick up Ammo for ranges, to fixing Humvee, handing out keys, linen, room assignments for barrack, filling out request forms to battalion for maintenance for barrack or furniture.

I met Oliver North in Kuwait before the invasion of Iraq. We were outside the Iraq border where forces were gathering to invade. We were going out on a recon mission and before we departed I ran into Mr. North. The group photo was taken just before we were crossing into Iraq to invade in 2003. I'm on the far left with my friends, each in charge of specific duties. Next to me is squad leader, Sgt. Balatico and Gunnery Sgt. Sawyer and Staff Sgt. Mc Duffie. I was in the invasion of Iraq and first to go into Fallujah in 2004. We were taking out the terrorists that were killing civilians. It was like the movie American Sniper. Chris Kyle was attached to our unit and provided over watch from terrorist snipers. We would also have look out posts just in case terrorist would try to come down the street. Our squad would go through houses to check for insurgents and weapons. One time I found an old Tommy gun. Our unit was the one who brought down the Sadam Statue. If you look up, 21 days to Baghdad or Devil Dog Diaries, that was my unit. It was a crazy day and there were a bunch of reporters in a hotel. They were so happy to see us after all the fighting and bombing. They said it brought them relief to finally see American Troops. The crowd began to gather around the statue trying to knock it over when our commander gave the order to bring it down.

As far as dealing with emotions relating to combat, witnessing casualties, and destruction, at the time I was more worried about staying alive but now it is very hard especially thinking of my friends that didn't make it back, one of who was lost in the city of Baghdad due to friendly fire.

There was one event that stands out where a van kept pulling forward even against our demands for it to stop, so we opened fire killing everyone in the van or so we thought until the door opened with a lady and man sticking their hands up in surrender. It was unbelievable that these terrorists used innocent people to kill us.

There was perhaps only one rare moment of normalcy when I was in Fallujah. We had not gotten supplied with MRE's so we went a couple of weeks without eating until we went out on patrol and came to house with some chickens who had eggs, and we found some potatoes as well as some oil. When we got back to our building we were held up in and our doc cooked up some eggs with potatoes. It was our moment of normalness in all the killing, fighting, and explosions going on, never knowing if we were going to make it to the next day...

My military experience has made me very appreciative on what we have today. It has taught me that being part of a brotherhood will have your back no matter what. I do feel guilty having made it back though when so many did not. I am sometimes cautious and jumpy in situations.

Today, I help out Post 9305 a Vietnam and global Veterans group with fundraisers and burial details for fallen warriors.

EPHESIANS 6:11-18

The Whole Armor of God

"Put on the whole armor of God,
that you may be able to stand
against the wiles of the devil.

Praying always with all prayer and
supplication in the Spirit,
being watchful to this end with all
perseverance and supplication for all
the saints --

DANI SIEBEN

U.S. ARMY
RESERVES

"THE PETALS OF THIS ROSE
ARE NOT EASILY WILTED."

My mother, Elizabeth Williams joined the Army reserves and served for few years.

My paternal uncle, Carl Crutchfield served as well. I have been in the U.S. Army for 10 years and a Drill Sergeant at Fort Jackson for over 2 years. The most rewarding aspect of being a drill instructor is that I have an opportunity to positively influence the new generation of the Army. I have a chance to groom tomorrow's Soldiers and influence their future leadership styles.

This picture is of my co-worker, D.S. West and myself and another picture showing me in the field teaching Soldiers how to react to contact battle drills.

I love seeing the Soldiers at the end of a cycle try and emulate me because they admire me, or the fact that they can execute any task I give them, not out of fear, but out of respect. I use my role to positively influence, motivate, inspire, and educate them. I enjoy the fact that I am the new Soldiers first real example of what the Army standard is. Being a drill instructor humbles me, because looking at the trainees, it reminds me of where I came from, and the fact that I used to be a private, and how I saw my drill sergeants as super heroes, and now there may be a young Soldier that sees me the same exact way. Motivation is a key aspect to the Soldier's physical discipline and is a critical aspect of training.

It brings me great joy to know that my Soldiers are graduating, despite of the hurdles that were before them, be it physical fitness issues, discipline, weight, etc. The fact that at the end of the cycle the Soldiers have made significant improvements, are now walking across the graduation field with their shoulders back, head up, and their chest out, makes me proud. I almost feel like a parent to 60 kids at a time, because I feel obligated to give them the best of me, to ensure that I draw out the best in them. I truly love this job and all the responsibility that comes with it. It is a blessing to influence so many lives and prepare them for possible deployments.

I suffered a great loss in 2008 and felt that I was alone in my time of bereavement. The loss of my mother was the driving force behind finally putting a book together. I never really had a chance to grieve and the book allowed me to take time and focus on my feelings.

I began to write down my feelings and shared my tears, anger, smiles and laughter with the world in my book, THE PETALS OF THIS ROSE ARE NOT EASILY WILTED.

There is so much that keeps me motivated about being a drill instructor, and I use it all to push me to be a better leader, Soldier, and overall person.

PSALM 23

The Lord the Shepherd of His People
A Psalm of David

The Lord is my shepherd; I shall not want.
He makes me lie down in green pastures;
He leads me beside the still waters. He
restores my soul;
He leads me in the paths of righteousness
For His name's sake.

Yea, though I walk through the valley of
The shadow of death. I will fear no evil;
For You are with me; Your rod and Your
staff, they comfort me;

You prepare a table before me in the
presence of my enemies; You anoint my
head with oil; My cup runs over.

Surely goodness and mercy shall follow me
All the days of my life; And I will dwell in
the house of the Lord
Forever.

AL ABBONDANZA

U.S. ARMY NATIONAL GUARD
IRAQ AND AFGHANISTAN

"USING YOUR WEAPON COULD BE ACCIDENTLY DEADLY."

During my college winter break, I enlisted in the Massachusetts Army National Guard January 1980 and earned my commission July of 1982.

This is a picture of myself on the first deployment in Iraq at Camp Speicher serving as a Civil-Affairs Officer in 2004. I was a logistics officer [major] at a corps support group [colonel level in command with 3000 Soldiers]. Due to a personnel change, I was assigned to cover the civil-affairs position within our unit. I am not a school trained civil affairs officer. I learned on the job, trial and error.

The picture shows us delivering aide. I carried an ax handle to shoo-away children that were getting too close or out of control. Using your weapon could be accidently deadly.

When people thank me for my service today, I feel humbled. I have a total of 30 years of service with 8½ years active duty in Italy (Ceggia and Vicenza), Guatemala, with 3 deployments to Iraq and 1 in Afghanistan. The remainder of service was the National Guard from 1980 to 1982 and Army Reserves for the balance of my service until retiring in 2010. This picture is of my second deployment with coalition officers in 2006 at Camp Delta, Al Kut, Iraq.

We had many indirect fire attacks in Iraq and Afghanistan. None were very close. But one RPG attacked a school complex in Tikrit in April of 2004. No one was injured. I was not scared during the attack, but afterwards while driving out of the area, we laughed about it in a nervous sort of way. There was a time we were driving south towards Tikrit, cresting a ridge on the highway and my driver and I saw a large pothole. We could not see inside it and drove over the pothole. I radioed the convoy about the pothole and to drive towards the right side. On the way back, heading north, the southbound traffic had been stopped. There was a large green disk in the pothole. It was a land mine. My driver and I had a long laugh. We had driven 'over' a landmine! Surviving the RPG attacks made me realize that the war was 'real'. The Soldiers that I served with and myself could have died. At point, I had no choice but to become an excellent small unit leader- utilizing all my NCOs in the mission planning and execution. Doing civil-affairs is not combat per se, but you have to be ready to engage the enemy, because if you look weak, they will engage you. You have to be 'tactically tactful'. Making a bad decision could get one of my Soldiers killed or wounded. I regret not being able to go back for more. I know my experience could help other Soldiers prepare for their deployments.

I stayed in touch with my family on a daily basis by sending emails. I sent a monthly email letter to my friends to keep them in the loop. But I never sent letters complaining or moaning about anything dangerous, which could have resulted being reported to the news. Soldiers of the 'Greatest Generation' returned home and suffered in silence and in many ways that continues today.

The picture is of my son, Andrew and myself in 2013. He is in the Army Reserves. I am a Life Member of the DAV. I utilized the Post 9/11 GI from 2012 to 2015, earning my MBA, CAGS and halfway through a MS in Nonprofit Management and recently started working for the Federal Government.

PSALM 35

The Lord the Avenger of His People

"This is my favorite because it is David's warrior prayer asking God to defend him against those who sought to tear him down. I wish I would have known this Psalm before I deployed."

MSGT ELDONNA LEWIS FERNANDEZ

U.S. AIR FORCE (Retired)
MIDDLE EAST

"IT SOUNDED LIKE AN ADVENTURE."

My name is Eldonna Lewis Fernandez.

I was born in Dallas, Texas and grew up in San Antonio. I was on my own attempting to figure out a path in life. One day I saw a commercial that said, "Air Force a Great Way of Life."

It sounded like an adventure to me. I enlisted in the Air Force and became a Contracts Specialist. The training was great and I adapted very well. I had no structure in my life prior to the service. I come from a family with a long tragic story set up for failure and bad choices. My mother died of alcoholism when I was only 12 years old and my father died emotionally afterwards and just sat on the couch drinking beer and smoking cigarettes. There was no parenting, no guidance, nothing. This resulted in my running with the wrong crowd and I dropped out of high school at age 16. My dad abandoned me when I was 18. I knew that I was going nowhere and fast. I got my GED and joined the Air Force. The discipline and regiment helped me thrive. I loved it and felt like I had a family and a place to belong.

I served from 1980 to 2003 and was stationed at MacDill AFB in Tampa, Florida, Bergstrom AFB in Austin, Texas, Davis Monthan AFB in Tucson, Arizona, RAF Lakenheth in the UK and Holloman AFB in New Mexico with deployments to Spain, Tunisia, and the Middle East after 9/11. My days were filled with a high paced environment that involved the purchasing and handling of contracts to keep the unit going and resupplied stateside and overseas. During actual deployments, we worked 18 plus hour days. The people that I met and experiences I had outside of the base were fantastic. This is a picture of one of the few friends I had while in the deployed environment. We were goofing around and having some fun.

Although I did not see actual combat and did not suffer any physical injuries, I did encounter psychological warfare with a man of the same rank as me because I wouldn't sleep with him. When he got there he decided and announced to me that he needed a hook up and I was it. When I did not comply he turned his troops and mine against me. Things would disappear off of my desk and he sabotaged my job and attempted to get me in trouble. He called headquarters and tried to report me for things or bring up situations to the commander. By the end of my tour I was a nervous wreck inside. My internal fear was that if I deployed again after that the same thing would occur and I would implode. I retired early as a result of this experience. I wanted to stay in the Air Force but couldn't fathom it after what I went through.

It was not until after I settled in and returned home that I began to realize how what had happened to me affected me. I felt dirty and couldn't retire fast enough. I spent the two weeks after my deployment scrubbing my house from top to bottom. I did not understand at the time that I was attempting to clean away what had happened. My friends back home expected me to continue life as normal. I knew that the United States was going to Iraq. But because of the negative experiences, I completed my papers to retire as soon as I could when I got back. I do not regret serving. The bad things, that happened were a blip on the screen of an outstanding career. I feel humbled and honored when people thank me for my service. I would ask everyone to never forget our sacrifices and understand that we will always grieve the loss of our time in the service.

The picture of me on my Harley was included in AARP Magazine for an article honoring our Veterans and taken by photographer Peter Yang. I have been a Harley rider for twenty years and riding is a healing tool for me. Not only do I feel free when I ride, it empowers me. If I didn't have my Harley when I was going through healing from the trauma from my life, I would not have been able to make it to the other side of the pain.

I never expected I would ever be a published author or professional speaker. I am both today. I was a contributing author in Heart of a Woman in Business and shared the idea with the creator of the Heart Book Series Sheryl Roush to co-author a book about military women called Heart of a Military Woman. Then I started speaking on "taking control of the handlebars of your life" and created the Go PINK Rules of Engagement and wrote the book on that. I really wanted to be a speaker and inspire people and transform lives. None of what I was doing was getting any traction and no one was taking me seriously as a speaker. I had branded myself as the Pink Biker Chic, which was only giving me small speaking opportunities in the motorcycling community. I got with a coach who helped position me with my expertise on contracts negotiation and Think Like A Negotiator was born.

Today I am a professional speaker and trainer, a Veteran owned business plus the Women Veterans ministry leader at my church. We have a small group that meets weekly and we make quarterly visits to the Veterans in the spinal ward at the Long Beach Veterans hospital. I am also an American Legion Member and help out where I can in the Veterans community.

My first published book is Think Like A Negotiator. My website is www.ThinkLikeANegotiator.com I am working on another book about the 10 Lessons to Lead an Engaged Life. I run my own 3-day trainings on negotiation and working on getting sponsors so Veterans can come at no cost. I want to empower Veterans to have the tools they need to lead an awesome empowered and engaged life.

Today I am a professional speaker and trainer, a Veteran owned business plus the Women Veterans ministry leader at my church. We have a small group that meets weekly and we make quarterly visits to the Veterans in the spinal ward at the Long Beach Veterans hospital. I have also started a non-profit to help eradicate poverty for women in a slum in Kenya. I went on a mission trip to Kenya and met the women of the Kipsongo slum who make beautiful handcrafted jewelry out of paper and beads. They have the joy of the Lord and are happy anyway despite their circumstances. I was led to invest in some of their beads and sell them with my book when I speak.

"Book and a Bead" is changing many lives and has led to the development of a non-profit and building a sustainable business for them through winning contracts for their beaded jewelry. The non-profit will also help put Veterans back to work as the manufacturing of the beads grows.

https://EldonnaLewisFernandez.com
https://BasketsandBeadsKenya.com

PSALM 23:4

Even though I walk through the valley of the shadow of death, I will fear no evil,
for you are with me;
Your rod and your staff, they comfort me.

ERIC LINKE

U.S. ARMY
AFGHANISTAN

*"WE NEED THAT STRENGTH
TO MAINTAIN PEACE."*

My great grandfather, Paul Mann served in the German army and was killed when Germany invaded Russia during WWII.

I joined the military after graduating high school and chose the army for a challenge. I always knew that I would be a Soldier, even at the young age of 4. My early days of training were tough. I was pushed to do my best after seeing other Soldiers pull weapons and encounter serious accidents while in training. If you got hurt, you were failed and sent home. I served from 1988 to 1992 at Ft. Ord, California, where I did tours in Panama, Columbia and Korea, where we did a two-week expedition for team spirit, a large simulated war. Just prior to leaving for active duty, I went to the LA riots in East Watts, L.A. When you are in the National Guard, it includes peacetime adventures too such as the Binghamton Floods to Florida hurricanes. The Army National Guard is what you make of it.

I was an aviation mechanic and later served with the National Guard in Rochester, New York, where I advanced to a CH-470 crew chief.

I was later deployed to Afghanistan 2006-2007. Our aircraft was shot at numerous times. We had many close calls. One particular event was when a Taliban Soldier planted IED's and killed American Soldiers. He was wounded and emotions flowed! War is an adrenaline rush. Every time that I returned safe, I thanked my brothers who did their job. We all kept each other safe.

We kept in touch with family and friends with letters, care packages and of course, we had Skype. But the worst part of war for me was when something went wrong at home, and although I knew what to do, I felt helpless. I remember a Soldier who found out that his wife was messing around while he was away. He shot himself. I'm not sure if it was out of love or embarrassment. It was not until after I returned home from deployment that my wife asked for a divorce. When I asked her why she had not let me know beforehand, she said that she wanted to wait for me to come home and tell me in person. I have a lot of respect for Grace in doing that. Many guys lost their focus when learning such news from a distance and not having any control over it.

I'm listed as a class 3 and suffer from hearing loss (tinnitus), a left ankle injury and degenerative disc disease on both lower back and neck, probably from carrying 150 lbs. for 4 years. I have tried to forget the emotions, the image of death, hurt, injuries and destruction over the years. But one never forgets the smell of death. As a Soldier, we sometimes self medicate to lose the memories of war and the bad times. After a bout of drinking and other factors and confronting myself on how I contributed to it all, I did some soul searching and obtained a degree in Theology to try to help me understand life. My wartime experience made me stronger and I learned to never fear anything again.

As of September 2018, I finally completed over 12 years active duty with the Army. We should never shut down our bases where we have been. Nor should we cut back on the military, as we need that strength to maintain peace. As for returning Soldiers, make sure your community adheres to their needs, whether social, psychological, emotional or financial.

I spend my time now doing small landscaping jobs with my son, Valor and teaching him to never give up on your dreams and that life is what you choose it will become.

PSALM 37:34

"Hope in the Lord and keep his way. He will exalt you to inherit the land; when the wicked are destroyed, you will see it."

KAT MORRIS

U.S. ARMY
IRAQ

"THE ARMY WAS ALWAYS MY FIRST CHOICE."

I was born in Weirton, West Virginia in 1965.

My dad was a Korean War Veteran. His brother my Uncle Roy Blankenship also served in the Korean War and was killed in action during the Battle of Pork Chop Hill. My maternal Grandfather Perry Strother fought in WWII, the Korean War and Vietnam. My cousin Billy Blankenship was in the Beirut barracks bombing, and my brothers Ralph Hartford in the Gulf

War with the U.S. Navy and brother Harold Blankenship OIF3. Many cousins and uncles also served. I was the first female in family that served in a combat overseas situation. Prior to serving, I was a single mom and bartender. I was a Sergeant in the U.S. Army and deployed with 630th transportation unit out of Little Washington, PA. I served as a 31K (communications) and an 88M heavy equipment operator and truck driver.

I remember that I was home with my kids and watching the news when we were attacked on 9/11. I headed to my reserve unit. I thought it was a red dawn scenario. I was pissed off. I joined to serve my country, and that is exactly what I did. The Army was always my first choice. Departure for training camp made my mom cry. It was tough, but the kids were awesome. I was 39 when I deployed and turned 40 shortly after arriving In-Country. I became "Mama Kat" to most of my unit. I was very determined that all those kids made it home alive and in one piece. I served in Operation Iraqi Freedom, Balad, Iraq from 2003 to 2005.

Those days were long, dusty and hot! This is Seth Pacifico and I in a transient tent somewhere in Iraq.

I was part of numerous convoys that were attacked by insurgents. Our camp was mortared on a weekly basis, convoys attacked with oil fires, small arms fire, mortars and IEDs. I was part of a very large convoy going to Jordon to pickup APC and tanks donated to new Iraqi government by Jordanian government. We were attacked close to the border by a marine gun Truck hit and we had to Life flight out casualties. Everything always happened so quickly, so you really just reacted by instinct. You had to keep moving and pray the kids weren't hurt. ITDs are what I dubbed the "improvised tripping devices" in our camps. There was plenty of them on a trip to the showers. I was always telling the kids to watch out for ITDs! Then one kid, Parinas, tripped over a tent guide wire and went down like a ton of bricks. I asked him why you kids never listen to mama and everyone started cracking up. This picture is of me somewhere in a transient tent in Iraq.

It was difficult being away from my kids and seeing the little Iraqi children suffering and lining the roads, begging for food and water. I constantly worried about the kids I deployed with. I was always fearful about them being maimed or killed. My brother died while I was in Iraq. I worried about my 18 year-old

Daughter who was pregnant with my first grandbaby, and all while she was caring for her two younger brothers while I was in Iraq. I tripped on an ITD while carrying 140 lbs. of gear across post to get to my truck. We were not allowed to bring trucks to the tents to load them. I injured my left hand, elbow and right knee. In November of 2003, I got extremely sick and was on quarters for two weeks.

This is a picture of my dear friend Harry Lewis, a fellow biker and Veteran. This was taken at the health and rehabilitation center of New Brighton in Minnesota, where he stayed just two weeks after getting a bypass surgery at the Minneapolis VA in September of 2014. He had no home or family.

I wanted him to come to Ohio and stay with my family. My husband, kids, siblings and grandkids all knew and loved Harry. But he refused to leave Minneapolis because he had so much faith in the VA there. I began traveling out there with financial assistance from my family to spend time with him, get him out to the movies, dinner and take care of him. He was diagnosed with fibrosis of the lung in September of 2015 and given 6 months to live. They just kept doing heart procedures on him. This was after years of going to the VA and complaining that he couldn't breath. He remained at the rehab from late September 2014 until May 9, 2017 when he died.

I have many severe health problems that continue to this day. The VA won't or can't give any explanation for illnesses. Maybe we should get rid of the VA altogether and get some real doctors. I'm moody and get upset easily with exaggerated startle response. I'm always tired, and hate large crowds. Things are not as enjoyable as they used to be. But the reception when I returned home was wonderful. My Legion had their honor guard there at my unit, when I got off the bus. My mama had a welcome home party for me down the river. It was strange though, as I had changed. My kids had changed. I was jittery and jumpy and stressed all the time. I couldn't find work, and there have been financial and health issues ever since. When people thank me for my service, I'm a little embarrassed. I don't really know what to say back to them. I keep in touch with many that I served with. My copilot, Sean Carver has visited my family and gone camping with us.

I feel that Obama pulling us out of Iraq was a crime. All of those Iraqi children that were slaughtered because of that haunts me to this day.

I am a member of the American Legion, a biker and a trucker.

PSALM 91 King James Version (KJV)

He that dwelleth in the secret place of the most High shall abide under the shadow of the Almighty.

MONTGOMERY J. GRANGER

MAJOR, U.S. ARMY (RET.)

"IT MADE FINDING A BATTLE RHYTHM DIFFICULT AT BEST."

My great, great grandfather served as an infantryman with the Union Army in the American Civil War. He left a diary of his time in the Civil War, which confirmed a Soldier's life is 99% boredom and 1% pure terror.

Various other relatives also served in the Civil War. My stepfather joined the U.S. Air Force and served in Korea during the early 1950s and my father was in the Navy during the late 1950s with my brother serving with the U.S. Air Force in Italy and Germany.

Dad told funny stories about being in the Navy, and my brother spoke in a limited way about his service. But my stepfather rarely mentioned his service. I spent 22 Years with the Army National Guard and Reserves in California and New York and retired in December 2008. I joined the California Army National Guard to serve my country, learn a valuable skill, and earn a little pay and to repay my college loans. My deployments were to Guantanamo Bay in 2002, Ft. Dix, New Jersey in 2003, and Iraq in 2004 to 2005. I was a Combat Medic for 5 years, Officer Candidate for 1 year, and a Medical Service Corps officer and Field Medical Assistant for 16 years.

I remember that day on September 11, 2001. As Director of Health, Physical Education, Athletics and Health Services, I was interviewing a school nurse. My secretary told me after the interview that a plane had hit the World Trade Center. I immediately thought of a pilot in a small plane having a heart attack or something. When the second plane hit I knew it was foul play, terrorism. I was called in to my unit, the 455th MP DET, in Uniondale, NY and spent seven days there in the Tactical Operations Center advising the Brigade Command on operations from my medical service perspective. No one knew what the hell was going on, but we were there and ready.

As a U.S. Army Reserve Captain, I found myself the ranking Army Medical Department officer in a joint military operation like no other before, taking care of terrorists and murderers just months after the horrors of September 11, 2001. My fellow Reservists and I ended up running the Joint Detainee Operations Group (JDOG) at Guantanamo Bay's infamous Camp X-Ray. I felt guilty about leaving my family and job back home. While in Guantanamo, I faced a myriad of torturous emotions and self-doubt, at once hating the inmates that I was nonetheless duty bound to care for and protect. But through long distance love, and much heartache, I found ways to maintain my sanity and dignity. I tell my personal story of that experience in my book, Saving Grace at Guantanamo Bay. At Gitmo, I would observe all new detainee arrivals from the airport on the Leeward side of the base, to in processing, to incarceration. On non-arrival days, I would attend daily detention hospital staff meetings held at Navy Fleet Hospital 20. Navy medical personnel cared for injured detainees. Many of the first detainees were coming straight from the battlefield in Afghanistan and had war wounds. The Army Military Police guarded the detainees. This was not a good mix. First, Navy medical personnel had zero experience or training in treatment of potentially dangerous and unlawful combatants. MP's had no experience dealing with injured detainees being treated by Navy medical personnel, who were treating detainees like any other sick or injured individual. A pen could become a weapon for a detainee. Detainees could obtain information from even casual conversation that could be used to disrupt operation. It took a lot of collaboration, professionalism and vigilance to keep things running safely and effectively. Turnover in personnel was frequent, and it made finding a battle rhythm difficult at best.

This picture shows a very tired Captain Granger inside our "Hootch", our home away from home at Abu Ghraib Prison, Abu Ghraib, Iraq during the winter of 2005. We inherited the hootch from the 418th MP BN. It was a mess when we got it and it took us weeks to neaten the place up. Notice the wall on the right, over my left shoulder. The hootch was an old prison cell and the painting was that of one of Saddam Hussein's prisoners.

My worst fear was being killed or wounded and not being able to come home to my wife and children. I did not want to be a burden to them. It was difficult being apart from my Hero wife and my children. They are the most important part of my life. These are my three boys I left behind in 2005. Left to right is pictured Harrison, Benjamin and Theodore wearing T-shirts I bought for them at Camp Victory PX in Baghdad, Iraq.

I am pictured here as then Captain Granger in April 2005 while on the road to Abu Ghraib to pick up my gear for reassignment to Ashraf, Iraq. One of the vehicles in our convoy got a bad flat. We stopped and everyone got out to pull security. I am pictured here in full battle-rattle and the way we dressed when outside the wire. My commander took the photo. I was promoted to major in February 2007. As for my reaction to combat, I call it an emotional train wreck. Taking care of bad guys is a collision between hatred and empathy. All the other stuff is just what it. You mourn your death before you get there. You mourn the death of your family. You accept death in order to function. Like the beginning of "Hurt Locker," war is a drug. Soldiering is a simple life. You don't worry about what to wear, where you are going, what you will be doing. This is because everywhere you are going, you are a target. If it happens, it happens. You do your job and if you wake up the next morning, you do it all over again. Those who couldn't function, or were panicked, hadn't accepted their own death.

In order to accomplish our goals for the protection of the US and allied interests and world peace, we need to stay in Iraq and Afghanistan and then lead a coalition for a Middle East Marshall Plan. The Global War on Terror is alive and well. Until all Islamists no longer have the means or will to kill us we must defend ourselves by any means necessary. As Aristotle said, "we make war that we may live in peace."

My reception coming back home was very good. We were praised for our service, honored, and I was asked to give a speech. It was euphoria retuning home and everybody was glad that I was home, until I began to recreate my role before I had left. Mommy was in charge of everything up until that point. She made all of the decision. It was challenging to get things "back to normal", except that "normal" was now changed forever. I was enraged by how everyone seemed to not know or care about the fact that there was a war going on. Then it hit me. That is why we serve, so that everyone else can go about their daily lives and not have to worry about the enemy. We serve so that everyone else can sleep at night. I have calmed down. But every once in a while I am back in Iraq, on a dusty road, scanning the landscape for IED's and out of place things that could kill me, but they are not there.

This is my whole brood and family with my wife Sandra, my personal Hero. It was taken in 2008 during Flag Day ceremony held by the local Elk's Club and sponsor of our Boy Scout Troop.

Today I am a public school district administrator, writer and author of other published works and wartime anthologies, such as Theodore and Operation homecoming: Iraq and Afghanistan and the Home Front in the words of U.S. Troops and their Families.

PSALM 55:22

Cast your cares on the Lord
And he will sustain you;
He will never let
The righteous be shaken.

JULIA MAKI PYRAH

U.S. NAVY

"I HAD NEVER FELT THAT KIND OF LONELY BEFORE."

I was born in Deer River, Minnesota.

Both of my grandfathers served in WWII, as well as a couple of my aunts and uncles. I was quite young when they all passed away. I wish now more than anything that I could have known my grandparents and have a conversation with them now that I am an adult.

My father was drafted for Vietnam but just days before he was about to ship off, they stopped the draft, and he did not have to go. I know he was relieved, of course, but he still has conversations about feeling guilty for not having to go, as a very close friend of his had to go and was killed. I suppose it is a different form of survivor's guilt.

I am the oldest of my siblings. At the time I left, I didn't know anyone that was in the military. Since then, my younger sister and her husband served. My husband, his brother, and most of my closest friends and their spouses have served. I enlisted the first time in 1997 and left for boot camp two weeks after graduating high school. I wanted to fly. The Navy recruiter was much nicer that the Air Force recruiter and promised me I could fly. It was as simple as that. Leaving my family was difficult. I found boot camp to be much harder mentally than physically. I felt like I was always in trouble and always getting yelled at. I'm a people pleaser, so separating from that was a challenge for me. I was also very lonely being away from family for the first time. I had never felt that kind of lonely before.

Once I was out of training and arrived at my actual squadron, I began to enjoy the Navy quite a bit. I adored flying and seeing the world from such a unique perspective. I enjoyed my travels and the opportunities that I was given. I completed training in Pensacola, Florida and Jacksonville, Florida during my first year. My first duty station was at VP-8 (Patrol Squadron) in Brunswick, Maine. That was our home base. From there we went on 6-month deployments to Iceland, Sicily, and Puerto Rico. We would be home for a year and gone for 6 months. This picture is of me with my P-3 crew-Combat Aircrew9, VP-8.

My days revolved around the flight schedule. When we were on home cycle, we were gearing up for our deployments and getting our crew qualified through flight simulators and our training flights to prepare. Each crewmember, was constantly working on getting qualified. When we weren't flying, or helping as an observer on a pilot training flight, we were studying, cleaning, or training other crewmembers. The things that probably changed me the most were witnessing poverty in other countries and to see the way others lived compared to us as well as the common comforts that we took for granted were unheard of in so many other places in the world. We as Americans live like kings and queens and do not even realize it. I got to know the Atlantic after staring at her for hundreds of hours from above. I had the privilege to know an entirely different world in the sky. It was peaceful, and beautiful.

Living a life around a flight schedule was difficult because you never knew if you would be flying a night or day flight until the day before. It made it difficult to schedule anything including college courses and being away from family was never easy. These were all of the reasons that I ultimately decided not to stay in the military as a career. I wanted to have a family, and these factors were not conducive to raising one. This picture is my now husband, AT2 Aaron Pyrah and I while we were in VP-8 together. My first enlistment lasted 5 years. I ended up getting out because I met my husband and we wanted to have a family. We knew it would be difficult to deploy and leave our little ones.

This may seem trivial to anyone who has been to war, but the day my entire crew failed the (simulated) Torpex event because

I failed to locate the submarine quick enough. I had let them down. I was humiliated and didn't know how I would face them the next day. But I did. I put one foot in front of the other and forced myself to go into work. And in the end, they forgave me, because that is what people do. I grew up in the military. When you are in that environment, you grow up quickly. I think you realize what is important in life, and how short it could be. I learned that there is a much bigger picture than the one I grew up in. Joining the Navy was the best thing I ever did.

Every time I returned from a deployment, I had more appreciation for America than I had ever anticipated. I wanted to shake people that complained about our free country. I wanted to scream and shout how good we have it here. I am thankful for those who display their patriotism and support for our troops. I would ask that all Americans not sit when the National Anthem is played and for those who complain that our country is oppressed, to stop. Some people have no idea what true oppression really is.

I am a member of the American Legion in my town and love to hang out with the older war veterans and listen to their stories. I have been a contractor for the government now since 2003. I am now a Technical Analyst on P-8s (the successor to the P-3s) for Foreign Military Sales. In June of 2017, 20 years after my enlistment into the Navy, I decided to reenlist in the DC Air National Guard. I am currently active as a reservist after a 15-year break in service working in Airfield Management with the ultimate goal of getting back in the air as a military flight attendant on C-40s. I always missed being a part of the military and flying. Now that my children are older and much more independent, I seized the opportunity when the 113th Wing was looking to fill flight attendant positions. I absolutely love being back and plan on retiring from the military when my service has been completed. It is not the conventional way to go, but nothing I've ever really done has been conventional.

I also enjoy working with Tactical 16, the VA, USO, Fisher House, Lone Survivor Foundation, Shepherds for Lost Sheep and other military support organizations and to provide any assistance I can through my books. I believe everyone has a cause, something inside of them that speaks to them and where they can best offer their services. I have found this to be mine.

In a way, I believe it is my way of continuing my service. I write stories for children of military Veterans and anyone else who enjoys an entertaining story. You can visit my published works at www.JuliaMaki.com

PSALM 139:14

I praise you because I am fearfully and wonderfully made; your works are wonderful, I know that full well

LEASHA WEST

US MARINE CORPS

"IT IS RARE TO MEET A FEMALE MARINE. THERE ARE VERY FEW OF US."

My specialized training was in weaponry as a Weapons Instructor.

My assignments included CBIRF (Chemical Biological Initial Response Force) and MCT (Marine Combat Training). I was responsible for the combat training of a 500 plus person training element in basic Marine Corps tactics and weaponry.

As a 10th generation military Veteran, my family traces it's military service back to the American Revolution. When I was growing up, I had the privilege of talking with multiple family members about their military service. My uncle, Barney Welch served with the Marine Corps and fought in Iwo Jima, Bouganville and Guam. He was the youngest Sergeant Major in Marine Corps history reaching the rank of E-9 at age 23. Uncle Barney passed in 2012 at the age of 93. Another uncle, age 82, served 12 years in the Army and was head of the Equestrian Division. When President Kennedy was assassinated, he was flown from Germany to Washington, D.C. to groom and shoe the horses that pulled President Kennedy's casket. He stayed up for 2 days and 2 nights perfecting every detail of each horse. Another uncle that served in the Marine Corps, age 76, was on a ship in 1961 preparing to invade Cuba during the Bay of Pigs. The ship was ordered back and he peacefully returned to the states. I also have 2 aunts that served in the Army that are still living. Based on my military heritage, I always wanted to be the first female Marine in my family to carry on our lineage of patriotic service in which I achieved.

This picture was a memorable day taken at Camp Geiger, NC with my boot camp sisters. We had just graduated Marine Combat Training and everyone was departing for individual MOS (military occupational specialty) schools.

I served my tour of duty stateside and never deployed overseas. An average day was up at 0400 as troops had to be in place at the weapons range and ready to fire at dawn. After shooting all day, I would hit the gym, lift weights and go for a run. In the evenings, I would square away my uniform and boots, do some reading and hit the rack around midnight.

This picture was taken when I was a student at Marine Combat Training where Marines spend 3 weeks in the field learning combat tactics and weaponry - the same place I returned and led students as an MCT Instructor. I am on the right returning from patrol.

There was one defining moment on the grenade range that has always stayed with me. As the Senior Weapons Instructor at MCT, I worked the live pits. There was one particular male Private who was fearful in the practice pits. Following 6 practice grenades, he was sent to the live pit and was the last student of the day. When he signaled he was ready, I handed him the grenade and he took it with confidence. Once I gave the order to *"pull pin"* he became visibly shaken, pulled the pin, assumed his stance to throw and DROPPED IT! By the Grace of God, I caught the grenade right before it hit the ground and I threw it with all my might. The grenade exploded in the air just as it cleared the berm. The look of terror in the Private's eyes is something I will never forget. He was dropped from MCT and discharged out of the Corps. I never saw him again, but to this day that near-death experience has haunted me.

My time in the service changed me in several ways. I developed a standard of excellence in all that I do and continue to raise the bar to this day. Most people who meet me or are around me commonly ask or guess that I am military. My most impressionable experience was with my drill instructors, MGySgt Danielle Hendges and GySgt Shirene Warner. They were both extremely tough and motivated me out of my mind! More importantly, they pushed me to be the very best version of myself. As a direct result of their training and guidance, I was the Honor Graduate and promoted to Lance Corporal (E-3) out of boot camp. From there, I reached the rank of Sgt (E-5) in less than 2 years, which is typically accomplished only after 4 plus years of service.

This picture is my promotion to Sergeant. It was such an unforgettable day! So many fellow Marines and former MCT students attended the ceremony. Subsequently, I have stayed in touch with many Marines that I served with as well as other Veterans I've met along the way.

When I returned home, I felt so loved and respected. Everyone was extremely proud and incredibly supportive. The community seemed fascinated, as it is rare to meet a female Marine. There are very few of us.

Today I am a business owner and professional speaker. Additionally, I have stayed involved with numerous Veteran organizations and currently sit on several boards. I authored the book RETIREMENT SAFEHOUSE and co-authored the books BEAT THE CURVE and MASTERS OF SUCCESS with Brian Tracy, and PERFORMANCE 360 with Sir Richard Branson. Other multi-author books include LEADERSHIP: THE FACULTY OF LEADERSHIP SPEAKERS ACADEMY AT WEST POINT and SUCCESS IS YOURS.

Psalm 144:1,2

Blessed be the Lord my strength
which teacheth my hands to war,
and my fingers to fight:

My goodness, and my fortress; my
high tower, and my deliverer; my
shield, and he in whom I trust; who
subdueth my people under me.

Nicolas "Neeks" Martinez

UNITED STATES MARINE CORPS
AFGHANISTAN

"MY LIFE'S NEW MISSION IS FOREVER DEDICATED TO HELPING OTHERS."

I was in the Active Duty Marine Corps from 2004 to 2009 and stationed in various places, but my main duty station was Jacksonville NC, on Camp Le Jeune North Carolina. I was assigned to 1st Battalion 6th Marine Regiment, a light infantry Battalion as a Communicator.

My Father was in the Military in Nicaragua during the overthrowing of Somoza with the Contras, and later came to the United States under political asylum. He joined the Army and has since retired.

Before the Marine Corps I was a troubled youth growing up in the streets of New York City. I rebelled and gave my mother a hard time. I emancipated myself, went to a military academy, graduated valedictorian at 16 and got my diploma from the governor, and later joined the Marine Corps, which shaped my perception of my world around me. It has continued to influence me as a man. The rest is history.

I lived for months on end in this vehicle during the most extreme of environments this world has while serving in Iraq and Afghanistan. I've driven them across thousands of miles of changing terrain, and had to critically maintain them with my brothers teaching me along the way. Like many Veterans, today and throughout history, at the end of my tour of duty I found it hard to make the transition back into civilian society. Combat changes you. I found it hard to gain employment. At interviews, I'd be asked about my experience. When I told them about my time in combat, their eyes would just glaze over. They weren't interested. All they cared about was what skills I had to offer the company. I've spoken to many Veterans since, only to discover they have had the same kind of issues—and then some!

When I enlisted in the Marine Corps in 2004 as an Infantry communications Marine, I never imagined that I would find myself in combat giving my brothers-and-sisters-in-arms haircuts in the most hostile and dangerous environments in the world. But that's where life took me.

These marines and comrades are resting in the haircut waiting line during 2008 in Afghanistan. I kept a visual log of these cuts, and the memories they bring are of both joy and sorrow. To this day, my battle buddies still track me down and reminisce with me about those "Combat Cuts". I remember how great they felt after a simple haircut, when most times we couldn't even get a shower.

I've been cutting hair for over 10 years at this point and have been splitting my time between upstate NY, and New York City with clientele of Veterans and civilians and events. I am also a NY state prison barber, and go to different prisons each month. This mobile ability not only exemplifies the novelty but also my mission of helping all walks of life by not being help down by brick and mortar. I have been on a bit of a sabbatical since my accident earlier this year and still recovering. I just started cutting hair again in August 2018. I still have my barber trailer. But the rig pulling it was what was taken. It's not finished yet, as I have been trying to stay focused on my healing. I haven't been to the VA to cut since I left the rehab/hospital. They want me back though… I miss being there for my family.

In my more ambitious moments, I see this as the beginning of a Movement: A call for not just Veterans but for all people who feel they've been squeezed into a tight spot. If we could all just learn to ask and offer each other help, we would be living in a Utopia. There would be no war, if we all simply helped each other. This is my life's new mission. I am forever dedicated to helping others. I was meant to do this. I'm proud to have people keeping our legacies alive so that the public can know, that we aren't social outcasts and war stricken monsters that could snap at any given moment. I've learned in my brief life on this earth that traumatic situations can be disabling to the mind, body and spirit. But once one learns to harness that fear and guilt into a force of positivity, and that the symptoms we call "PTSD" are not in fact a disability, but a superhuman ability that has evolved into having extra honed sensory awareness, we have won.

With your help, I can start doing my part to change the world—to wake people up and start a nonviolent revolution—one haircut at a time...

A Lakota chief and Korean/Vietnam Marine, Chief Leonard "Crow-Dog" Singer wrote the following. He took me under his wing and taught me this and many other things.

"Warriors are the ones that bear the weight of the people, that translation is the same in any warrior based indigenous society. You were predestined to do this, because you were made strong enough to from birth.."

Thank you all. Semper Fidelis.

Psalm 23 King James Version (KJV)

23 **T**he Lord is my shepherd; I shall not want.

2 He maketh me to lie down in green pastures: he leadeth me beside the still waters.

3 He restoreth my soul: he leadeth me in the paths of righteousness for his name's sake.

Erika Luna Tharp

US ARMY NATIONAL GUARD

"MY MOTHER ALWAYS BELIEVED IN ME AND KEPT ME MOTIVATED."

I was born in the Dominican Republic and was the first in my family to join the military.

Prior to joining the Army, I was working my Medical Assisting degree. I chose the Army because it was the one I noticed had the most benefits. School was my main priority at the time and I wanted to finish college and have a back up plan after the military. It was hard to leave my family but I was excited. I felt scared the first couple of days at training but everyone was wide eyed just like me. My mother always believed in me and kept me motivated. Not many people would join the military with the chance of leaving loved ones for long periods of time. I wrote tons of letters to stay connected with family.

I served in the National Guard from 2007 to 2014. We did a lot of accountability with tools and parts for aircrafts and vehicles. I was primarily responsible for supervising and performing management of warehouse functions in order to maintain equipment records and parts and accountability for all tools. I developed a sense of accomplishment. I loved the job. It was a great experience and I became proficient in my duties.

This is a picture of my friends and comrades who reminded me of home. They were warm and down to earth human beings. They all had one goal and that was success in all aspects of the word. They were my comrades and my family.

Today I am working on Masters in teaching and the proud mother of a new baby boy. My husband, David is now serving with the 101st Airborne just like his WWII Veteran grandfather and Gulf War Veteran father did, both whom have passed. His brother, Aaron is serving with the US Air Force.

I always said that I'd never get married or have kids... I guess someone was really laughing at me when I was planning out my life, knowing they already had a plan for me.

2 Corinthians 4:16-18:

So we do not lose heart. Though our outer self is wasting away, our inner self is being renewed day by day. For this light momentary affliction is preparing for us an eternal weight of glory beyond all comparison, as we look not to the things that are seen, but to the things that are unseen. For the things that are seen are transient, but the things that are unseen are eternal.

Made in United States
North Haven, CT
01 December 2021

11817046R00169